DISCIPLESHIP

Author
Richard J. Reichert

BROWN-ROA
A Division of Harcourt Brace & Company

A Division of Harcourt Brace & Company

O u r   M i s s i o n

The primary mission of BROWN-ROA is to provide the
Catholic and Christian educational markets with the
highest quality catechetical print and media resources.
The content of these resources reflects the best insights
of current theology, methodology, and pedagogical research.
The resources are practical and easy to use, designed to meet
expressed market needs, and written to reflect the
teachings of the Catholic Church.

Nihil Obstat

Rev. Richard L. Schaefer

Imprimatur

✠ Most. Rev. Jerome Hanus, O.S.B.

Archbishop of Dubuque

January 4, 1998

Feast of Saint Elizabeth Ann Seton

The Imprimatur is an official declaration that a book or pamphlet is free of doctrinal or moral error. No
implication is contained therein that anyone who granted the Imprimatur agrees with the contents,
opinions, or statements expressed.

Illustrations—Rob Suggs

Photo Credits

Mimi Forsyth—46, 73: Robert Fried—40, 55, 74; Robert Cushman Hayes—32, 48, 85; James L. Shaffer—18,
28, 39, 44, 68, 69, 77, 81, 90; Jim Whitmer—2, 7, 8, 16, 23, 25, 36, 53, 62, 83

Printed in the United States of America

ISBN 0-15-950467-8

10

What's it all about?

Introduction
The tools of discipleship

Dear reader,

To be a disciple in today's world, you are called to live your life as Jesus instructed. To accomplish this goal, the following commitments are required from you:

1. Believing in yourself

Jesus' second great commandment is "Love your neighbor as yourself." (Matthew 22:39) In order to do this, we must first know how to love ourselves. Chapter 1 helps you understand what a treasure you are to God and what it means to believe in yourself.

2. Relating to your parents

At this point in your life, your relationship with your parents or guardians is changing and growing. This can be both an exciting and an unsettling time for everyone. Knowing that your parents are people, too, chapter 2 aims to help you better understand them and relate to them.

3. Choosing your friends

In Rules of Civility, George Washington stated, "Associate yourself with people of good quality if you esteem your own reputation, for 'tis better to be alone than in bad company." His advice still holds true today. Chapter 3 looks at the importance of choosing your friends wisely and how to stand up against the harmful pressures of your peers.

4. Growing in your faith

As you grow physically, mentally, and emotionally, it is also important to grow spiritually. This involves developing an awareness of God's presence in your life and learning to take time for prayer and service. Chapter 4 focuses on striving to achieve this spiritual maturity.

5. Understanding the value of sexuality

God trusts you to use the gift of your sexuality in a mature and responsible way. Indeed, it is a precious gift to be treasured.

Because we live in an "Everybody's doing it!" society, chapter 5 helps you understand the importance of knowing the real meaning and value of your sexuality.

6. Making positive choices

During this time in your life, it is likely that you will be faced with the choice of whether or not to use drugs, including alcohol. Since the reason many youth use drugs is to escape their troubles or to fit in, it is important for you to learn how to make positive choices. Chapter 6 addresses the issues surrounding drug use and abuse and then offers you many reasons why saying "no" is the wisest choice.

7. Learning to act justly

As a disciple of Jesus, you work with God's kingdom whenever you follow the words and example of Jesus. The kingdom of God is God's reign of perfect peace, love, and justice. Chapter 7 explains how you can act as a disciple of Jesus, working to challenge injustices in our world today.

8. Accepting challenges

Chapter 8 guides you in writing your autobiography. Include your successes and failures. Add your personal stories that brought you joy, pain, humor, and tears. Incorporate your growing knowledge of faith and of the Church. All of your experiences are an important part of your story that can lead to a happy ending with God in eternity.

By committing to live a life according to the eight principles presented in this text, you will have the necessary skills to face the challenges of adolescence. The skills you will acquire throughout this course will give you the essential tools to live a life of discipleship, a life according to how Jesus instructed his followers to live. Best of luck!

Dick Reichert
Green Bay, Wisconsin

Chapter 1

Believing in Yourself

Discovering the good

Using magazines, cut out words and pictures that you feel say something positive about yourself. Glue these items in the picture frame below. Be sure to include examples that describe your personality, talents, and physical being. Don't be shy—you have a lot of GOOD to discover!

Share this "portrait" of yourself with the class.

 THE NOTED QUOTED

"You are a wonderful, worthy, and lovable person.
Appreciate that about yourself.
No one has ever been, or ever will be, quite like you.
You are an individual, an original,
and all those things that make you uniquely you
are deserving of love and praise."
                                                —Peter McWilliams

You are somebody

Everyone has a very basic need deep inside to feel special, unique—to be a somebody. During this time in your life, this need to feel unique is probably very strong, perhaps the strongest it will ever be. Many teenagers want to express themselves in creative ways but fear they will stand out too much or be thought of as "different." They want to feel special, not odd.

As you grow in many ways, your image of yourself also changes. These teen years of your life can be filled with excitement and confusion. Yet throughout the entire growth process, you can definitely count on one thing—God has created you as a special person, a somebody.

No two human beings are exactly the same, no matter how much we may seem alike. Jesus tells us that the very hairs on your head are numbered by God and that your name is written on the palm of God's hand. You are somebody. That's how God made you. No one else is quite like you, and in God's eyes, you are irreplaceable. You always have been and always will be special. It's as simple as that.

 Share your view

Name someone in your life who has made you feel very special. How did he or she do this?

 THE NOTED QUOTED

"No one like you was ever born or ever will be."
—Constance Foster

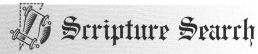 # Scripture Search

"See, I have inscribed you on the palms of my hands...." (Isaiah 49:16)

On the hands below, write your name. Then use each letter of your name to begin a word or phrase that states one thing you love about yourself.

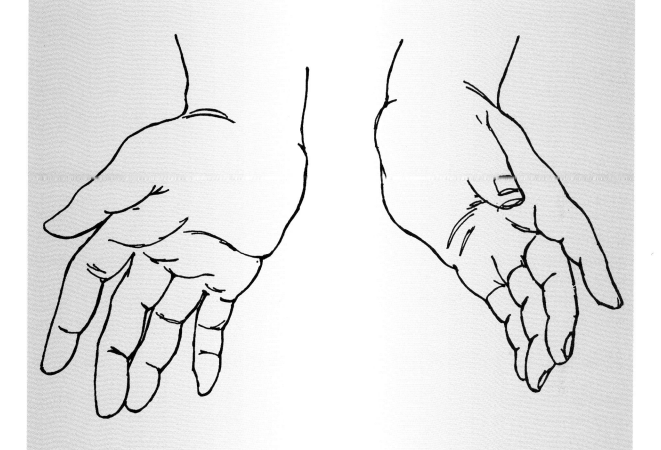

As a disciple, you are called to believe these proclamations about yourself. You are called to love and accept yourself, especially during these years of change.

Catechism Clip

Being in the image of God the human individual possesses the dignity of a person, who is not just something, but someone. . . . (357)

How come I don't always feel like a somebody?

This is a valid question. The answer has to do with how worth is measured. Some people measure others only by what is on the outside; they are mainly concerned with physical appearance—the clothes we wear, the color of our skin, the shape of our bodies. Such people also often use numbers to measure worth—how much money we have, our IQs, how fast we run, our test scores.

This system of measurement is okay to some degree, although it should not be an important factor when we measure our own self-worth. For example, it might be fun to know who in your class is the fastest runner. Perhaps you are the tallest student in your class, or you may be the only one with red hair. Even though these things make you unique from others, remember that just being yourself makes you a somebody.

Unfortunately, believing in yourself can be difficult at times, especially if people measure you against your peers. When you feel that you aren't what others expect, take comfort in knowing you are always precious to God.

It is what's inside that counts the most

What makes you unique, the one-of-a-kind somebody you are, can't be measured with numbers or seen with the naked eye. It is what's inside you that counts the most. To discover this, you must be willing to look beyond externals and beyond numbers. It takes great faith to make this self-examination. God lovingly created you and knows your inner person, the real you. Your parents and true friends also know and love the real you.

So even if you can't yet name or even recognize what makes you special and unique—a one-of-a-kind somebody—you can believe that you are special and unique. You have God's word. And you can trust your parents and friends—the people who know you best.

Believing in yourself keeps you from always trying to measure up to other people's ever-changing standards. Instead, you can measure yourself according to the constant standards of discipleship, how well you follow the words and example of Jesus.

List three people who you feel are very comfortable with their uniqueness. How do you think they achieved this?

_____

_____

_____

But everything's changing!

During these years of your life, many things are changing. You are no longer a child. Instead, you are experiencing new feelings, gaining new friendships, and watching your body grow.

You're probably not sure what you can do, what you want to do, or what you should do. Most of the same feelings and emotions of childhood are there, such as anger, fear, excitement, and love for your parents. But all of a sudden you have to find new ways to express these feelings. At age four, being scared and letting people know you were scared was easy. But how do you express your fears at age thirteen or fourteen? Telling your parents

you love them and accepting their love was easy when you were seven years old. Now it may be awkward or embarrassing for you to tell or show your parents just how much you love them.

Friendships are changing too. When you were a child, your friends were those children with whom you played. For a teenager, being friends and having friends becomes a major concern. "Do people like me?" "What do they say about me?" These questions are important, and yet, you may not know the answers.

During this time, your body also may be rapidly changing. For example, your feet seem to grow on their own schedule,

ignoring the rest of your body. Or suddenly you are six inches taller, and you don't know how to control your longer legs. Or the opposite can happen—you may not seem to be growing at all when everyone else in your class is.

At this point in your life, it is normal to feel confused, self-conscious, or worried. It is often comforting to remember that all of your peers are going through this same process. As these changes happen, it is especially important to continue to believe you are somebody.

List one thing about yourself that you would like to change. Why would you make this change? How would this change alter the way you feel about yourself?

_____

_____

_____

_____

Some assembly required

Coming into adulthood is much like purchasing a new bike; both require some assembly. All the pieces of your adult self are already within you, but it's going to take some assembling on your part. You have intelligence, special talents, freedom, a full range of emotions and feelings. And you have limits and weaknesses, too.

It is the unique combination of these gifts and limits you possess that makes you a special somebody. But how do you get all these parts working together? How do you go about discovering and developing your talents? How do you know what your freedoms are?

Fortunately, like a new bike, there are instructions to follow for forming your adult self. As Catholics, we can draw on the Ten Commandments, the law of love, and the teachings of the Church to help us make good decisions. There is still some trial and error—testing this, trying that. Of course you can also get good advice from parents, teachers, and other adults. They've already been through the assembly process. But in the long run, you are responsible for your own decisions.

This process of "putting yourself together" is both exciting and scary. Know that you are not alone. Your parents and friends support you. And God always believes in you and in who you are becoming. With his grace, God provides the strength and help you need.

A CELEBRATION OF ADULTHOOD

In a group of three, develop a "rite of initiation" for our society that could be used to mark the transition from youth to adulthood.

• Describe the ceremony.

_____

_____

_____

_____

• Who would lead the ritual?

_____

_____

• What objects or symbols would you use in the rite? What's the significance of these objects?

_____

_____

_____

Called to be a disciple

Believing in yourself is a continual process. Each chapter in this text looks at a specific area in your life that is connected to this belief—relating to your parents, choosing your friends, growing in your faith, understanding your sexuality, making choices, learning to act justly, and accepting new challenges.

But in addition to knowing you are a somebody, God also asks you to recognize that you are continually called to be a disciple and that you have an eternal destiny. This call was established by your Baptism into the Church. Each chapter offers you ways of living out your discipleship as a growing Christian in today's world.

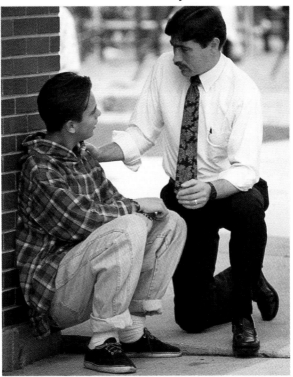

 For which one of your talents would you like to be famous? How could you use your talent and your fame to help others grow in their own faith?

_____

_____

_____

_____

THE NOTED QUOTED

"What we must decide is how we are valuable, rather than how valuable we are."
—Edgar Freidenburg

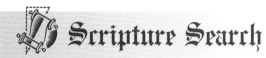

Scripture Search

Read 1 Samuel 16:7. Reflecting on this verse, answer the following questions.

1. Do you think our world looks at a person's appearance or into his or her heart?

2. What are some ideas on how people could look into each other's hearts?

3. What is one thing about your heart that you wish others would notice more often?

4. How does the verse from the book of Samuel connect with the following quote by the fox in the story *The Little Prince* by Antoine de Saint-Exupéry?

"It is only with the heart that one can see rightly; what is essential is invisible to the eye."

Reflection

Reader #1: "Can a woman forget her nursing child, or show no compassion for the child of her womb? Even these may forget, yet I will not forget you. See, I have inscribed you on the palms of my hands . . ." (Isaiah 49:15–16)

Reader #2: Lord, help me remember that you have made me a special, unique person and that I am a somebody.

Reader #3: Help me be patient as I grow through these changing years in my life.

Reader #4: Help me hear your call to be a disciple throughout my life.

Leader: In your name, we pray.

All: Amen.

HOMEWORK

There is no question about it—God has created you as a special, unique person! Take time now to read Psalm 139:1–18. To help you remember how incredibly you were created, summarize each of the sections in your own words.

• Psalm 139:1–6

• Psalm 139:7–12

• Psalm 139:13–18

Chapter 2
Relating to Your Parents
 Can we talk?

Relating to your parents or guardians may not always be easy. There are certain topics that adolescents feel comfortable discussing with their parents or guardians and other topics that make teens uneasy. Fill in the following chart with your personal ideas and experiences.

Topics I feel comfortable discussing	Topics that make me uneasy

 Share your view

Discuss the following questions with your classmates.

1. Which topics do you think teens are most comfortable discussing?
2. Which topics make teens feel uneasy? Why are these subjects difficult to discuss with a parent or guardian?
3. What could help make communication easier?
4. Through your own experience, when have you found to be the best times to talk with your parents or guardians?

Why can relating be so difficult?

At times, many teenagers experience difficulty relating to their parents or guardians. The reason is simple enough to see; however, dealing with it can be another matter. Here's the situation. Adolescents feel a need to break away from childhood. You are no longer helpless and may feel a strong desire to take more control over your life, to make decisions for yourself, to do more things on your own. Because of this desire for more responsibility, it can be very upsetting when people continue to treat you as if you are still a helpless child.

That's where your parents come in. For many years, they have known you primarily as their "baby." The fact is, until recently, you really were small and rather helpless in many areas of your life. You needed them to care for you, to make decisions for you, and to protect you from harm. In fact, in some areas of your life, you still need their help, their protection, and the wisdom of their decisions.

For just a minute, put yourself in your parents' or guardians' position. They have been thinking of you as a child for many years. Their habits of thinking and acting toward you can't change overnight. They need time to adjust to the "new you." Understanding their position may help you be more patient with the process of learning new ways to communicate with each other.

You are indeed at an "in-between" stage in life. You are growing out of your childhood ways of communicating with your parents but are not yet able to discuss with them on an adult-to-adult level. The challenge? Finding ways to communicate with which both you and your parents are comfortable!

 THE NOTED QUOTED

"Adolescence is a period of rapid changes. Between the ages of 12 and 17, for example, a parent ages as much as 20 years."

—*Changing Times*

List five favorite qualities of your family.

_____

_____

_____

_____

_____

There's more to it

Contrary to how you may be feeling, your parents or guardians don't really want you to remain in childhood forever. More than anything, they want you to be healthy—free from physical danger and illness—and happy—filled with joy and enthusiasm for life.

Throughout your childhood, it was necessary for your parents to watch over you and to make decisions for you to ensure your health and happiness. As a child, you were content to let them make these decisions.

But now you want to take more control over your life and make more of these decisions yourself. You have your own ideas about what will make you healthy and happy. Because of this, you need to communicate your ideas to your parents in a way that both you and your parents will understand.

So two things may begin to happen. First, you and your parents may start disagreeing about what is "good for you." Second, even when you agree with your parents, it may seem to you that they are still treating you as a baby if they continue making decisions for you.

Here's the challenge: You need to let your actions demonstrate to your parents that you really are outgrowing your "baby" ways. One way to do this is by using a simple formula called GROW.

G = gratitude

R = responsibility

O = obedience

W – work

GROW stands for four qualities that you need to exhibit as you become more mature. By showing your parents that you are "GROWing," they are much more likely to allow you to make some of your own decisions for staying healthy and happy. Let's look at each of these qualities and what they mean for you.

Gratitude

Small children tend to take a great deal for granted. They simply expect that there will always be clean clothes in the dresser, food on the table, toys in the toy box. They expect someone to pick them up when they fall or be there when they need help or want to be entertained.

Small children do not realize how much time and energy it takes on their parents' part to meet their needs. Parents have the responsibility to meet the physical and spiritual needs of their children. Most parents do so out of love.

If you want your parents or guardians to know you are maturing, one of the quickest ways to show your maturity is to be grateful for all that they do for you. Showing your gratitude is so simple—tell them "thank you" often.

 ## Catechism Clip

Respect for parents (*filial piety*) derives from *gratitude* toward those who, by the gift of life, their love and their work, have brought their children into the world and enabled them to grow in stature, wisdom, and grace. . . . (2215)

In what ways do you think your family is a "holy" family?

_____

_____

_____

 ## Scripture Search

In your Bible, read the story of how Jesus cured the ten lepers (Luke 17:11–19). Answer the following questions.

1. How does this story show gratitude?

2. What are five things your parents or guardians do for you for which you are grateful?

3. What are some clever ways in which you could tell your parents or guardians "thank you"?

Share your answers with the class.

 # A round of applause

Create a thank-you note for your parents or guardians. In the card, specify five things for which you are grateful. Place the note in a place where your parents will be surprised to find it (for example, in the medicine cabinet, on their desk, in the mailbox, in their briefcase).

Responsibility

Responsibility is simply your "ability" to "respond" in an appropriate manner in a given situation. Little children need a lot of direction to act responsibly. But as you grow older, you gain more control of your life and of the events that occur in your life. You have the ability to choose how you respond to what happens. In order for adults to know you are not a "child" any longer, they need to see you act in responsible ways.

How can you show that you are a responsible person?

• Take good care of your things, including your clothes and valuable possessions, such as your bike or stereo.
• Be on time.
• When asked to do something, do it right away.
• Get your homework done on time.
• Clean up after yourself.
• Keep your room neat.
• Get up in the morning on time.

As you are making decisions, anticipate the effects of your actions as best you can. If you promise to do something, follow up on it. Show that you can be relied upon to do the right thing without having to be told several times.

You are not alone in this. God gives you the strength, or grace, to walk in right relationship with him and with one another. Personal prayer and participation in the sacraments will help you in living a responsible life.

 ## Scripture Search

One situation that allows you to show your responsibility is when you are on your own or supervising others. Read the parable of the talents in Matthew 25:14–30 and listen to what Jesus says about being responsible. In class, discuss your answers to the following questions.

1. Which servant did Jesus say was the most responsible? Why?

2. Describe a time in your life when you acted very responsibly.

3. Describe a time in your life when you could have been more responsible.

4. What is one way in which you plan to show your parents or guardians that you are a responsible person?

Sign on the dotted line

Complete the "contract" on page 97. By signing this contract, you commit to showing your parents your ability to be a responsible person. In order to fulfill the agreement, you need to develop a plan describing how you will display your responsibility and outline the plan on the contract. When finished, sign and date the contract. Then cut out the page and display it where both you and your parents or guardians can see it.

Obedience

The fourth commandment tells us to honor our parents. According to this commandment, parents and guardians are called to represent God in the family. Because we live in an imperfect world, not all parents are perfect, nor are all children. We are called to do the best we can.

Obedience is more than just following rules. Children are capable of following rules. But on the adult level, to obey also means understanding the reason behind the rule and knowing why rules must be followed. An example of adult obedience may involve a rule regarding curfew. "Child" obedience would mean you would be home on time. "Adult" obedience is knowing why the appointed time is best (you need your sleep, a city curfew, etc.) and why it is important to be home by that time (don't want your parents to worry, show of responsibility, etc.).

 THE NOTED QUOTED

"Imagination is something that sits up with Dad and Mom the first time their child stays out late."
—Lane Olinghouse

Just as important, obedience means to trust and respect the person who established the rule. Jesus obeyed his Father in all things, even when that required great sacrifice. Jesus' disciples obeyed him because they realized he loved them and knew what was good for them. They didn't obey him out of fear or because they had no choice in the matter. Rather, they sought his advice and asked for help in making decisions.

If you want to demonstrate to your parents that you are ready to make your own decisions, the quickest way to do so is to show that you understand their rules and that you appreciate their advice.

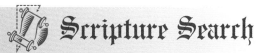 # Scripture Search

In your Bible, read the story of the wedding in Cana (John 2:1–11) and answer the following questions.

1. How does this story show Jesus' obedience to his mother?

2. What do you think would have happened if Jesus had disobeyed Mary?

3. What is one rule in your home that you need to obey more effectively than you do now? How do you plan to improve your obedience?

 ## May I have your attention, please?

Write a short letter to a small child explaining to him or her why it is important to be obedient. Be sure to give the child some examples of what it means to be obedient.

Dear _____ ,

_____

_____

_____

_____

_____

Signed,

_____

What rules do you now follow that you will have your own children follow also? Why are these rules important?

_____

_____

_____

Work

As you desire to take more control of your decisions for health and happiness, you must also take responsibility for a share of the work in the family. Your parents or guardians are not your servants and should not have to do everything that needs to be done. Growing up means being willing to do what you are asked to do and, more importantly, to notice what needs to be done and to do it without being asked.

Nothing pleases parents more than to see their child help out and do chores without having to be told and without hearing any complaints. Is your job to do the dishes? Take out the garbage? Do the laundry? Clean the bathroom? Baby-sit your younger brother or sister? Then do it! Do it on time. Do it well. Do it cheerfully. This will convince your parents very quickly that you want to be treated more maturely.

Here's another tip—volunteer. If you see that your mom or dad is really tired or busy, offer to do more than your assigned tasks. Ask if you can help out in some way to make life easier for them. The goal isn't to gain "brownie" points. As you grow older, you will learn that mature people simply offer their assistance when they see someone in need.

 ## Scripture Search

Jesus wasn't afraid to work or to serve others. He often saw other people's needs and did what he could to help. Read the story about Jesus washing the feet of his disciples (John 13:1–11). When you are finished, discuss the following questions in class.

1. What work was Jesus not afraid to do?

2. What work in your home are you not afraid to do?

3. How can you improve your attitude about the work you do not like to do?

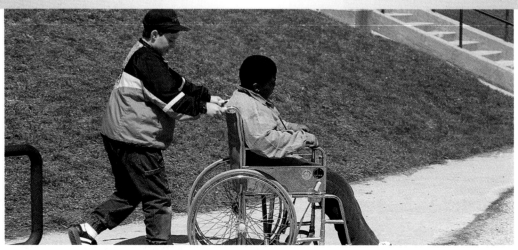

So much to do, so little time

If you were in charge of assigning the work in your house, how would you divide the household tasks among your family members? Below, list your family members in column one and then create a "to do" list in column two for each person. Be sure to include yourself! When you are finished, be ready to discuss your family members' tasks and the reasons behind your decisions.

Family members   **Tasks "to do"**

If you could do one thing for your entire family, what would it be?

_____

_____

_____

Putting it all together

Being willing to GROW will show your parents or guardians that you want to be treated more like an adult. Showing gratitude and responsibility, being obedient, and completing work is difficult to do all of the time. What's important is that you try to develop these more adultlike qualities. If your parents see you being more grateful or acting more responsibly, the message will be loud and clear—their "baby" is growing up. Your parents will almost instinctively begin to treat you in a more mature way.

Becoming adult is a trial-and-error process for both you and your parents. You'll both make mistakes. Your need to be treated in a more adult way is becoming very strong right now. It's what you feel will make you happy. Your parents' need to make sure you are safe and happy is just as strong. You and

your parents won't always agree on what will make you safe and happy. Disagreements are bound to happen during this "in-between" stage you are entering.

A sure way to help your parents or guardians realize you deserve to be treated in a more adult way is to demonstrate that you are becoming more adultlike in your actions. This means being more grateful, responsible, obedient, and willing to share the work.

Finally, parents and guardians are also people with needs, fears, and personal interests. Recognizing and respecting your parents' needs and interests is a key to understanding why they act the way they do. Understanding them is a key to getting along with them. The ability to understand others is also a sure sign that you are becoming an adult!

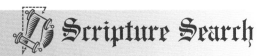

Scripture Search

Read Sirach 3:1–16. Choose two verses from the passage and write them below. Then write a short paragraph for each verse reflecting on how the message of the verse applies to your life experiences.

Verse 1:   Verse 2:

Reflection: Reflection:

Reflection

Read the following prayer together as a class.

> *Jesus,*
>
> *Help me be more grateful for everything I am given and for everything my parents do for me.*
>
> *Help me be responsible in my words and actions.*
>
> *Help me be obedient to my parents and respect their rules and decisions.*
>
> *Help me do my work with a positive attitude.*
>
> *Amen.*

HOMEWORK

Family Prayer

> *God made us a family.*
> *We need one another.*
> *We love one another.*
> *We forgive one another.*
> *We work together.*
> *Together we follow God's word.*

> *Together we grow in Christ.*
> *Together we love all people.*
> *Together we serve our God.*
> *Together we hope for heaven.*
> *These are our hopes and ideals.*
> *Help us attain them, O God,*
> *Through Jesus Christ our Lord.*

Choose at least two lines from this prayer that you feel describe your family. Give specific reasons for your choices.

Chapter 3
Choosing Your Friends
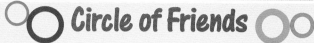 Circle of Friends

Your friends are the circle of people who allow you to be yourself and who love you for who you are. True friends encourage you to be your best self. List your friends' names around the circle below. Then, within the circle, list all the things you have in common with them. Include what you like to do together, activities you're involved in, and your similar personality traits.

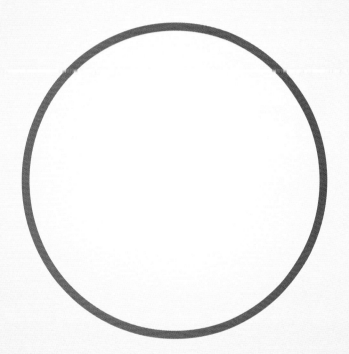

Briefly describe your group of friends. Tell what is special about each person in the group.

_____

_____

_____

_____

_____

 THE NOTED
QUOTED

"I am so thankful to God for giving me such kind friends to hold me by the hand while I am passing through my life."
—Lydia Maria Child

People who need people

Peer means an "equal," someone similar to you in age, education, training, or social status. For you, this includes your classmates and your friends. During adolescence, your peers begin to play a new, very important role in your life.

Up to now, your parents have been the main source of information about "who you are." They've also been the most important people in your life. During this in-between stage, you begin to rely less on your parents and depend more on your peers to find out about yourself. This doesn't mean you should stop listening to your parents and pay attention only to your peers. It just means you need peers and parents to be able to continue to grow in self-understanding and self-worth.

You need to continue to expand your world beyond your immediate family and to learn how to be yourself in the bigger world. You need the sharing, the views, and the reactions of others as well as your parents and family. In short, you need people.

 ## Getting to know you

There are many different ways to meet new people. In the space below, list a few of your friends. After each name, write where or how you met this friend.

1. What would you say is the "oddest" way you ever made a friend?

_____

_____

2. Where and how do you imagine you'll meet your next new friend?

_____

_____

 ## THE NOTED QUOTED

"Friendship? Yes, please."

—Charles Dickens

As you become involved in a wider range of activities, your group of peers will grow. Besides school, you may meet new people at dance classes or swimming lessons, sporting events or summer camps. During this time, your horizons are expanding beyond your family. In fact, spending time with your peers at this point in your life becomes very important. You need to "test out" the person you have grown to be. Learning to get along with your peers is a major part of the maturing process.

As your peer group grows, you will have many people with whom you can choose to be friends. Not all of your peers will be your friends. In fact, some peers may pressure you to be someone or to do something with which you are not comfortable. True friends respect you. They never ask you to go against your religious beliefs or moral values. It is important to choose your friends carefully.

As George Washington, first president of the United States, once said, "Associate yourself with people of good quality if you esteem your own reputation, for 'tis better to be alone than in bad company."

 THE NOTED QUOTED

"A friend is one who knows you as you are, understands where you've been, accepts who you've become, and still, gently, invites you to grow."
—Ralph Waldo Emerson

How have your friendships changed over the years?

_____

_____

_____

_____

Friends are special peers

All your peers can help you learn more about what makes you the unique somebody you are. But your friends, the special peers in your life, play the most important role of all. In this in-between stage, friends do what your parents did when you were a baby and a small child. They play a significant role in helping you discover and believe that you are somebody.

But what is a friend? What makes a person a friend and not just a peer? The following explanation of FRIEND may help you understand and remember exactly what a friend is.

THE NOTED QUOTED

"Friendships multiply joys and divide griefs."
—H.G. Bohn

Catechism Clip

Chastity is expressed notably in friendship with one's neighbor. Whether it develops between persons of the same or opposite sex, friendship represents a great good for all. It leads to spiritual communion. (2347)

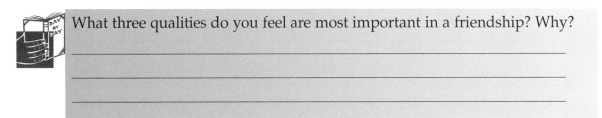

What three qualities do you feel are most important in a friendship? Why?

_____

_____

_____

F = Fun. Friends are people with whom you have fun. They make you laugh. You aren't bored when you are with them, even when you aren't doing anything special. Whatever you do, be it chores or homework, seems to be more fun when you do it with a friend. Having fun together is often what begins a friendship.

R = Reliable. Friends can be trusted. They keep their promises and your secrets. They're loyal, willing to drop what they're doing to help you when you need them. They put up with your moods, your failures, your limits. They don't say, "I'll be your friend as long as you . . ." or "if you . . ." Real friends simply say, "I am your friend no matter what, through thick and thin." Jesus taught us that this unconditional love is what friendship is really all about.

THE NOTED QUOTED

"A friend is one before whom I may think aloud."
—Ralph Waldo Emerson

I = Interested. Friends usually share a number of similar interests. That's part of the reason they are fun. They like the same music, movies, sports, or school subjects. They like spending their free time together. But that's only part of it. Real friends are also deeply interested in you—the whole you. They are interested in everything that affects you or is important to you. They share your excitement, your tears, your successes.

E = Encouraging. Real friends encourage you. They give you courage to face the tough things in life. Friends help you become more responsible. They help you deal with failure and help you accept your limits and weaknesses without feeling sorry for yourself.

N = Noticing. Real friends notice. They notice and are concerned when you are feeling down. They notice when you're worried. They notice the things you like and the things that bug you. They notice when you need help. You don't have to ask a real friend for much—a real friend notices and starts helping before you can ask.

D = Durable. Finally, a real friendship lasts. Sure, you'll have disagreements with a real friend. But real friends are always willing to make amends. A real friendship stands the test of time.

How important is forgiveness between friends?

_____

_____

_____

_____

 THE NOTED QUOTED

"We are each of us angels with only one wing. And we can only fly embracing each other."
—Luciano de Crescenzo

 Friendship is . . .

Finish the following sentences about your friends.

• The most fun I've ever had with my friends was _____

_____

• I know my friends are reliable because one time _____

_____

• My friends and I are most interested in _____

• One area in which I encourage my friends is _____

• I am thankful that one time a friend noticed I _____

_____

• The friend I've known the longest is _____

A special gift

Who wouldn't want a friend like the ideal one just described? Although no friend can always be perfect, real friends have all of these qualities to some degree. How do you make friends like that?

THE NOTED QUOTED

"A true friend is the greatest of all blessings . . ."
—La Rochefoucauld

You develop friends by being friendly and having fun. You try to be reliable and show an interest in others. You encourage and help others. You notice what is important to someone else. You respect others and treat them like the special somebody they are.

You have to be yourself. A friend is someone who recognizes the real you, the unique somebody you are. Don't try to be someone you are not. The real you is the best you. As you continue to meet new people and look for more friends, be patient. Real friends are a gift!

THE NOTED QUOTED

"A friend is a present you give yourself."
—Robert Louis Stevenson

Pressure from your peers

The desire to "fit in" is very strong during this time in your life. You want to feel accepted and to have friends. Your peers also want this. Thus, many teens are easily swayed and influenced by the opinions and suggestions of their peers. This peer pressure can be either positive or negative. Your goal should be to recognize the positive pressures and not to be a "pushover" for the negative ones.

Positive peer pressure is harmless enough. If everyone is wearing jeans to the dance, you may decide to wear them too. If your teammates go out for pizza after the game, you may decide to join them. There are negative peer pressures, though, that try to push you into doing things with which you are not comfortable or that could cause you harm. How can you tell when routine peer pressure moves into more serious areas? How can you identify the "pushers"?

THE NOTED QUOTED

"And, of all the best things upon earth, I hold that a faithful friend is the best."
—Edward Bulwer-Lytton

Harmful peer pressure can be recognized by four qualities:

P = Panic

U = Use

S = Shame

H = Hurt

Panic. If someone asks you to do something and you immediately feel a sense of panic, it is likely the person is using negative peer pressure. Such people want you to compromise your own beliefs to go along with theirs, and rightly enough, this causes you to panic. When you feel this way, it is best to say "No, thanks!" and walk away.

Use. Peer "pushers" tend to use others for their own advantage. Real friends help, support, and have a sincere interest in what is good for you. But when peer pressure is harmful, another person uses you to make himself or herself feel good. "Pushers" have no interest in how their actions affect you. They only want to use you to make themselves look or feel better.

Shame. "Pushers" like to shame you into doing what they want you to do. Phrases such as "You're such a chicken!" or "What are you, mommy's baby?" can make you feel like you need to prove yourself to fit in with the group. You don't want to be considered a coward or a baby. When people have to use these kinds of shame tactics to get you to join them, you can be sure that what they want you to do is harmful to you or to others.

Hurt. Harmful peer pressure always hurts. It hurts emotionally by putting negative labels on those outside of the group. It hurts your sense of self-worth. If the pressure pushes you into using drugs or having sex, it hurts you physically. Most importantly, when you act against your conscience and do what you know is wrong, it hurts you spiritually.

 THE NOTED QUOTED

"I destroy my enemy when I make him my friend."
—Abraham Lincoln

✂ *Catechism Clip*

Anyone who uses the power at his disposal in such a way that it leads others to do wrong becomes guilty of scandal and responsible for the evil that he has directly or indirectly encouraged. "Temptations to sin are sure to come; but woe to him by whom they come!" [Lk *17:1*] (2287)

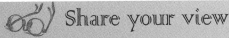
In a group of four, discuss the following questions. When finished, share your group's responses with the class.

1. What are the greatest negative pressures facing teens today?

2. What are the best ways to avoid negative pressures?

3. What are examples of positive pressures?

Believe in yourself

To be able to resist harmful peer pressure and the "pushers" who use it on you, you need to believe that it's okay not to go along with a group, to be an individual. The more you believe in yourself, the less power the "pushers" have over you. As long as you have a sense of self-worth and believe you are a somebody, you will be able to withstand negative pressures. If you know what you believe in and stand for, you will be less tempted to give in to negative pressures. You will also be less likely to become a "pusher" yourself.

 THE NOTED QUOTED

"Hold a true friend with both your hands."
—Nigerian proverb

Which qualities within yourself make you a good friend?

_____

_____

_____

_____

Come on, everyone else is doing it

Rate the degree to which you think there is peer pressure in your school or neighborhood to engage in each of the following activities.

	No Pressure					Very Strong Pressure
Try drugs	1	2	3	4	5	6
Use alcohol	1	2	3	4	5	6
Smoke	1	2	3	4	5	6
Be sexually active	1	2	3	4	5	6
Cheat in school	1	2	3	4	5	6
Shoplift	1	2	3	4	5	6
Other _____	1	2	3	4	5	6

Compare your ratings with other students in your class. Discuss any differences.

Choose wisely

As your world of peers grows, you continue to choose who to include in your circle of friends. Choose people who are fun, reliable, interested in who you are, encouraging, concerned about you, and durable. Remember, not all peers will be your friends—some may want to "push" you in negative ways. Choose wisely.

 ### THE NOTED QUOTED

"Life is to be fortified by many friendships. To love, and to be loved, is the greatest happiness of existence."

—Sydney Smith

 ## Scripture Search

"Faithful friends are a sturdy shelter;
whoever finds one has found a treasure.
Faithful friends are beyond price,
no amount can balance their worth."
—Sirach 6:14-15

1. The Book of Sirach says that "Faithful friends are a sturdy shelter." What new image would you use to describe friendship?

2. How can you measure the "worth" of friendship?

3. What is one thing you "treasure" about your friends?

Reflection

Leader: Lord, we thank you for our friends and the love they give to us. We now listen to Jesus' words about friendship.

Reader #1: "As the Father has loved me, so I have loved you; abide in my love. If you keep my commandments, you will abide in my love, just as I have kept my Father's commandments and abide in his love (John 15:9–10).

Reader #2: "I have said these things to you so that my joy may be in you, and that your joy may be complete. This is my commandment, that you love one another as I have loved you (John 15:11–12).

Reader #3: "No one has greater love than this, to lay down one's life for one's friends. You are my friends if you do what I command you. I do not call you servants any longer, because the servant does not know what the master is doing; but I have called you friends, because I have made known to you everything that I have heard from my Father (John 15:13–15).

Reader #4: "You did not choose me but I chose you. And I appointed you to go and bear fruit, fruit that will last, so that the Father will give you whatever you ask him in my name. I am giving you these commands so that you may love one another" (John 15:16–17).

Leader: Lord, you have taught us to love one another. Help us choose our friends wisely. Teach us to be friends to one another. In your name, we pray.

All: Amen.

Design an advertisement with the theme "Friend Wanted." Be sure your ad includes the qualities you are looking for in a friend, the activities you would like to share, and the "benefits" you can offer in return.

Chapter 4
Growing in Your Faith

 Keeping fit

Imagine having the following telephone conversation with God.

(Ring! Ring!)

Student: Hello?

God: Hi, there! How have you been?

Student: I'm fine, but who is this?

God: I'm God, your Creator.

Student: Wow! Really? This is so cool!

God: I was just wondering how you are.

Student: What do you mean?

God: I mean, I was wondering if you are keeping all sides of yourself in shape.

Student: All sides?

God: Yes! Let's talk about them one at a time.

Student: Okay.

God: How are you keeping your physical self in shape?

Student: That's an easy one! I'm on the basketball team, I walk to school, and I try to eat balanced meals.

God: Good for you! Now how about the emotional side of yourself?

Student: Well, I have good friends who listen to me when I have a problem and try to help, and I try to laugh a lot every day and not take life too seriously.

God: Again, well done! How about the intellectual side of yourself?

Student: I do my best in school, and in my spare time, I do crossword puzzles or read a book.

God: You are doing a fine job of keeping many sides of yourself in shape. Now for the last one—how do you keep the spiritual side of yourself in shape?

Student: Well, I . . .

 How do you keep the following sides of yourself in shape?
- physical _____
- emotional _____
- intellectual _____

Share your ideas with the class.

My spiritual side?

As a human being created in God's image, you have many sides to your personality—physical, emotional, intellectual, and spiritual. You can easily see and understand how you are growing physically (your body is maturing), emotionally (your feelings are stronger and deeper), and intellectually (you continue to advance in school). But what does it mean to grow spiritually? The spiritual side of yourself is your faith, how you keep in touch with God, how you pray.

It is easy to focus on the physical, emotional, and intellectual growing that is occurring during these years of your life. The challenge is to develop your spiritual side as well. This is best accomplished through prayer.

Name one person who you feel has deep faith. What spiritual qualities do you admire about him or her?

_____

_____

Defining prayer

Prayer is the time you spend focusing on God's presence in your life, your relationship with God, and your relationships with other people. It does not need to be formal, memorized, or spoken aloud. The way you pray is personal. In your lifetime, you will have the opportunity to pray in many ways. Find the method that works best for you.

One of the best ways to begin developing your spiritual side is by noticing—really noticing—the wonders of the world around you. Take a close look at a kitten, the flower growing in a pot by the window, a bird in a nearby tree, a drop of water. Each is a miracle in its own right, filled with life and wonderfully assembled.

Stop for a moment and examine your hand. Turn it over and move the fingers one by one. Look at your nails and your fingerprints—unique in all the world! Think of everything your hand does—writes your name, pats someone on the back, waves to a friend. The possibilities are endless.

You are a walking, living miracle, a masterpiece of craftsmanship and genius. All around you are other kinds of miracles, proof of God's work in the world. Do you want to know more about God? Begin to notice—really notice—what God has created. And remember, all the miracles of creation were created by God.

When you take the time to examine God's creation, you can't help but notice and experience God in the process. That's praying—the first step in developing the spiritual side of your nature.

Catechism Clip ✂

"[Jesus] was praying in a certain place and when he had ceased, one of his disciples said to him, 'Lord, teach us to pray.'" *[Lk 11:1]* In seeing the Master at prayer the disciple of Christ also wants to pray. By contemplating and hearing the Son, the master of prayer, the children learn to pray to the Father. (2601)

THE NOTED QUOTED

"A prayer in its simplest definition is merely a wish turned Godward."

—Phillips Brooks

How and when does your family pray together?

_____

_____

_____

Where do I go from here?

As you continue to develop your prayer life, you may find yourself asking the following questions:

When should I pray?

Where should I pray?

How should I pray?

What should I say?

Why should I pray?

Although you will eventually develop a prayer style that best suits your needs and time schedule, the ideas in the following sections will help you get started.

When should I pray?

You pray whenever you take time to notice God's presence in the world or focus upon your relationships with God and others. Thus, prayer can happen at any time. When you wake up in the morning and thank God for another day, that's prayer. When you sit down to a meal and take a moment to bless the food, that's prayer. When you ask God to give you wisdom as you take a test, or ask God to give comfort to your sick grandmother, or praise God for the joy of your new nephew, that's all prayer. You can talk to God at any point or at every point in your day.

The key is to find at least one time during your day to spend in prayer, talking to and listening to God. It may be the first thing you do in the morning. It could be your last thoughts before falling asleep at night. It may be while walking to school or riding the bus, during study hall, or in your room after school.

Choose a particular time in your day to set aside for prayer. You can always pray at other times, but "reserve" one time to focus on God's presence in your life. Once you've done this for a while, taking time for prayer will be a natural part of your day, as natural as brushing your teeth!

Where should I pray?

Because prayer can happen at any time, it can also happen at any place. The key is to choose a place where you won't have a lot of distractions. Find a quiet place away from the TV or radio. Even though you can pray on a noisy school bus, as you begin to develop your spiritual side, it is best to find a more quiet, reflective place to pray.

Perhaps for you this place will be in your bedroom or in your favorite chair in the family room (choose a time when no one else is there). You may find a place outdoors or decide to stop in at your church each day. Wherever you choose to spend this time, know that God is there.

. . . [Jesus] would withdraw to deserted places and pray.

—Luke 5:16

Jesus often felt a need to go to a quiet place to pray. Where can you go to be alone to pray?

_____

_____

_____

How should I pray?

There are many ways to pray. The key is to find the one method of prayer that helps you focus on your relationship with God. Trying many different ways of prayer will help you narrow down your choices to the methods you like best. Use the following ideas to get started.

1. **Formal prayers.** Some people like to pray the prayers that they learned as a child or that they have memorized from use. Such prayers may include the Lord's Prayer, the Hail Mary, the Rosary, or the Act of Contrition.

One prayer that I learned as a child was

_____

I like this prayer because _____

_____

_____

_____

2. **Conversations with God.** This type of prayer allows you simply to talk to God as you would with any other friend. Share with God how your day is going, ways in which you want to improve, your dreams, and your feelings.

🦉 THE NOTED QUOTED

"Prayer is conversation with God."
—Saint Clement of Alexandria

3. **Journaling.** If you like to write, this method of prayer may work very well for you. Start a notebook, and during your prayer time, write a letter to God. Using a journal is a great way to tell God what you're feeling in your heart, what's happening in your life, or to ask God for strength and guidance.

4. **Reading and studying the Bible.** If you enjoy reading, this type of prayer may be most meaningful for you. Choose a short passage from a book in the Bible and then reflect on its significance in relation to your own life.

When reading the Bible, we turn to God as our inspiration, providing us with the guidance and the strength we need to overcome many of life's difficulties. On pages 99 and 101 in the appendix of this book, you will find numerous biblical references to read during particular times in your life. These inspirational cards can be cut out and carried with you or placed in your Bible for easy reference. At some time, you may wish to give one of the cards to a friend who is in need of God's guidance. On the blank card, feel free to write in one of your favorite Bible passages that you can read when you need strength and guidance.

5. **Spending time in nature.** Many people find it easy to focus on God when they spend time outdoors, enjoying the blessings of God's creation. Going for a walk or sitting near a tree is a good time to reflect on the wonders and miracles of God.

6. **Being still.** If you feel your days are so full of activity, maybe your best means of prayer would be to set aside some time to relax. Perhaps playing soft instrumental music will calm you and slow you down so you are able to focus on God's presence in your life.

🦉 THE NOTED QUOTED

"I have so much to do that I must spend several hours in prayer before I am able to do it."
—John Wesley

7. **Service.** For some people, prayer happens when they are being of service to others. This could be time you spend talking to an elderly neighbor or running errands for a person who is homebound. As you help someone else, it is easy to thank God for the blessings in your own life.

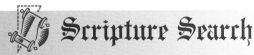
Scripture Search

Read chapter 11, verses 1–4, from the Gospel of Luke in which Jesus teaches his disciples the Lord's Prayer. Then answer the following questions.

1. How can you keep the Lord's name "hallowed," which means holy?

2. How do you envision the Lord's kingdom?

3. How easy is it for you to forgive others? To have others forgive you?

What should I say?

Prayer is how you converse with God. Your prayers are often offered to God in one of the following five forms: blessing or adoration, petition, intercession, thanksgiving, praise.

In the prayer of blessing or adoration, we bless God who has blessed us. Every day of your life you see the many blessings God has bestowed upon the world. Look all around you and take time to delight in all the gifts given to us by God the Father. You may wish to respond with a simple prayer from your heart, blessing God for the gifts you enjoy.

Petition is when we ask God for the important things we need. One thing we ask God for is forgiveness. Another prayer of petition is to ask that God's kingdom come. Every need can become a prayer of petition, including asking God to be with your family as you travel or to be with you during a busy day.

In the prayer of intercession, we ask God for something on the behalf of others. We must intercede on the behalf of our friends, as well as our enemies. You may ask God to be with a friend who is feeling depressed or with your grandmother who is recovering from a stroke.

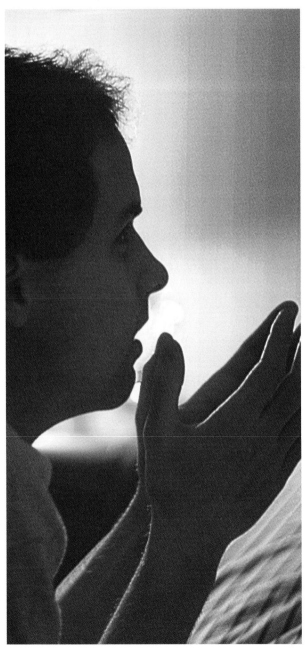

Corporal Works of Mercy

There are an endless number of people in our world today who are in need of our prayers of intercession. Read Matthew 25:35–46. The Corporal Works of Mercy is a list of seven good works that identify people who are in need of our prayers. For each work of mercy, write a short prayer of intercession asking for God's love and protection for these people.

• Feed the hungry.

• Give drink to the thirsty.

• Clothe the naked.

• Shelter the homeless.

• Visit the sick and imprisoned.

• Ransom (free) the captives.

• Bury the dead.

THE NOTED QUOTED

"If you pray for another, you will be helped yourself."

—Yiddish proverb

Thanksgiving is when you take a moment to thank God for the gift of life and all its blessings. You may thank God for a day off from school, the love of your family, or the daily food on your family's table.

With the prayer of praise, we honor and glorify God, who has shared all goodness with us. Praise is recognizing the endless wonders that God has created. When you notice the world around you and all its marvels, you are called to praise God.

Share your view

We are called to give thanks for everything the Lord has created. Read Daniel 3:59–81. Then list three of your own blessings in the following prayer of praise.

_____ , bless the Lord;
praise and exalt the Lord above all forever.
_____ , bless the Lord;
praise and exalt the Lord above all forever.
_____ , bless the Lord;
praise and exalt the Lord above all forever.

Catechism Clip

"Prayer is the raising of one's mind and heart to God or the requesting of good things from God" (St. John Damascene, *De fide orth.* 3, 24: PG 94, 1089C). (2590)

Why should I pray?

Prayer is time for you to center on God the Father's presence, Jesus' example, and the Spirit's guidance in your life. Prayer helps you notice the joy and good in the world around you. Prayer helps you make sense of what is happening in your life. Taking time every day for prayer allows you to be more at peace.

 Scripture Search

As a class, read Colossians 1:9–14. Then in small groups, rewrite these verses in your own words. Use your newly-created prayers as the opening and closing prayers for upcoming classes.

_____

_____

_____

_____

_____

_____

 THE NOTED QUOTED

"Pray to God in the storm—but keep on rowing."
—Danish proverb

Describe a time when God answered your prayers.

_____

_____

_____

_____

Remember, you are not alone

The best way to develop the spiritual side of yourself is through prayer. Where, when, and how you decide to pray is up to you. But it is very important that you choose a time and a place that helps you focus on God's presence in your life. After all, every one of us has many reasons to praise, petition, bless, and thank God.

Of course, prayer is not always an individual action. The whole community gathers to pray together during Mass, or when performing an act of service, or when participating in the sacraments. These forms of communal prayer will enhance and make your own personal prayer time more meaningful. By taking the time for both individual and communal prayer, your spiritual side will be in good shape!

Now let's go back to the opening conversation with God.

God: How do you keep the spiritual side of yourself in shape?
Student: Well, I . . .

After reading the chapter, how would you now answer God's question about how you keep your spiritual side in shape?

_____

_____

_____

_____

_____

Scripture Search

Prayer is powerful! Read and summarize below what Jesus taught his disciples about prayer in Matthew 7:7–11.

Reflection

Leader: Let us pray.

Reader #1: *I got up early one morning*
And rushed right into the day;
I had so much to accomplish
That I didn't have time to pray.

Reader #2: *Problems just tumbled about me,*
And heavier came each task;
"Why doesn't God help me?" I wondered.
He answered, "You didn't ask."

Reader #3: *I wanted to see joy and beauty,*
But the day toiled on gray and bleak;
I wondered why God didn't show me.
He said, "But you didn't seek."

Reader #4: *I tried to come into God's presence;*
I used all my keys in the lock.
God gently and lovingly chided,
"My child, you didn't knock."

Reader #5: *I woke up early this morning,*
And paused before entering the day;
I had so much to accomplish
That I had to take time to pray.
("The Difference," author unknown)

Leader: Lord, teach us to be prayerful people. Help us spend time with you every day. In your name, we pray.

All: Amen.

HOMEWORK

Choosing a special time and place to pray helps you develop your spiritual self. Create your very own customized prayer plan by completing the following statements.

• The best time of the day for my daily prayer is _____

_____

• My personal place for daily prayer is _____

_____

• Two ways to pray that I want to try are _____

_____

_____

• I would like to praise God for _____

_____

_____

• I would like to petition God to _____

_____

_____

• I would like to thank God for _____

_____

_____

• I feel I need to take time to pray because _____

_____

_____

In prayer it is better to have a heart without words, than words
without a heart.
—John Bunyan

From your heart, write your own prayer of petition, praise, blessing, thanksgiving, or intercession. Then use this prayer every day as part of your daily prayer.

_____

_____

_____

_____

_____

Chapter 5
Understanding the Value of Sexuality
Life's many treasures

Undoubtedly, you possess items that you treasure. Some of these treasures may be reminders of your childhood, such as your first doll or truck. Others may be more recent possessions, such as a diary or an A paper on which you worked very hard. Perhaps you have items that were given to you when someone passed away—a medal worn by a grandparent or a photograph of your ancestors. Your parents may even have saved some of your early artwork or clothing because—for them—they are treasures.

What makes an item a treasure? For many people, treasured items are priceless and irreplaceable. The items may be stored in a box, but the memories associated with them are stored in our hearts, filled with love. Losing life's treasures or having to give them away is unimaginable.

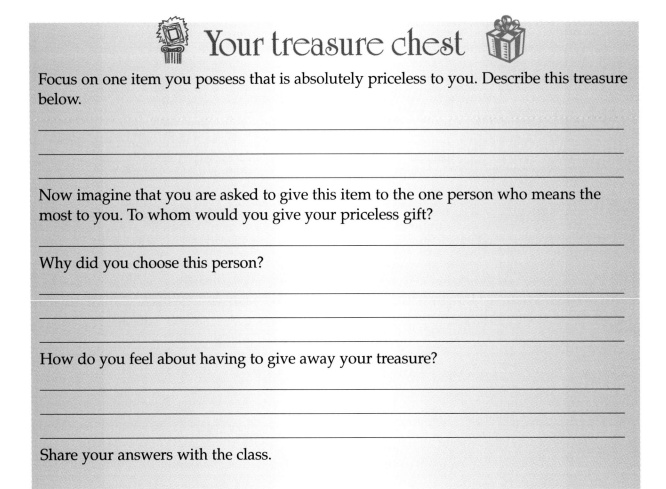

Your treasure chest

Focus on one item you possess that is absolutely priceless to you. Describe this treasure below.

_____

_____

_____

Now imagine that you are asked to give this item to the one person who means the most to you. To whom would you give your priceless gift?

_____

Why did you choose this person?

_____

_____

How do you feel about having to give away your treasure?

_____

_____

_____

Share your answers with the class.

Starting point

This chapter aims to better your understanding of the value of you sexuality. As a person of faith, you know that sexuality is much more than being able to label the anatomy or knowing how conception takes place. It's more than talking about diseases such as AIDS and syphilis that are or can be sexually-transmitted. It's more than knowing what happens to a person physically and emotionally during puberty. You already have these facts, or you will learn this information in other courses. This knowledge is obviously necessary for your well-being, but not nearly as important as knowing the value, the *gift*, of your sexuality.

 THE NOTED QUOTED

"Sexuality throws no light upon love, but only through love can we learn to understand sexuality."
—Eugen Rosenstock-Huessy

Catechism Clip

"Love is the fundamental and innate vocation of every human being" (*FC* 11). (2392)

Name some of your role models who help you understand the value of your sexuality. How do they model this value for you?

_____

_____

_____

_____

_____

_____

_____

_____

God believes in you

Your sexuality is a gift given to you by God, a powerful gift that is to be treasured. Through your sexuality, God shares with you the awesome, mind-boggling power to bring a new person into existence. God trusts you to use this gift wisely. God is confident that you are old enough to appreciate this awesome gift, that you will respect this power, and that you will deal with it in a mature, responsible way.

Now think about this—laws do not permit you to drive a car alone until you are at least sixteen. You are not given the responsibility of voting wisely until you are eighteen. Your parents are still not ready to allow you to decide your own curfew. Yet God is willing to entrust you with the power to bring new people into existence! God believes in your ability to know the value of your sexuality. God trusts you.

Knowing God believes in you will help you make wise choices regarding your sexuality. Understanding that God trusts you with the greatest power of all—the ability to cocreate human life—will give you the strength to treasure the gift of your sexuality. As a young person, you will be pressured to be careless about your sexuality, to forget that God trusts you to say "no" to sex before marriage. Yet as a young Christian, you know that "doing what is right" is so much more important than simply "doing it."

 THE NOTED QUOTED

"The most important thought I ever had was that of my individual responsibility to God."
—Daniel Webster

It's about being friends for life

Once you understand the gift of your sexuality, you also discover when and with whom the gift should be shared. Think back to the opening activity where you could give your priceless treasure to only one person. You wanted to make sure this was a person who would also find value in your gift, someone who would treasure the item as much as you did. You were very careful to choose wisely.

The gift of your sexuality is also priceless. Knowing this, you do not want to give it away to just anyone. The gift of sexuality is to be shared with one very special friend. This is the intention of the Sacrament of Marriage. This special friendship between a man and a woman is so strong and so unselfish that both people are willing to give themselves totally to the other for a lifetime commitment. It is only in this lifelong friendship that the use of our power to create new human life makes full sense. It is only in marriage that this gift of self to another person expresses the kind of love that understands the value of sexuality.

Abstaining from sexual intercourse until you have celebrated your commitment in marriage shows that you value the trust God has placed in you. You know God believes in you, and you are willing to live up to the responsibility of saying "no" until you have said "yes" to a lifelong friendship in marriage.

🦉 THE NOTED QUOTED

"Success in marriage is more than finding the right person; it is a matter of being the right person."
—Rabbi B.R. Brickner

Write a short prayer asking for God's guidance to help you abstain from sex until marriage.

_____

_____

_____

_____

Scripture Search

Jesus forgives us for what we have done wrong. Read John 8:3–11 and answer the following questions.

1. For what does Jesus forgive the woman?

2. What does Jesus challenge the woman to do now?

3. What can this story teach us today?

Meanwhile . . .

As a teenager, you know marriage is still many years away. This allows you the time to understand yourself and the gift of your own sexuality before you choose the person with whom you are going to make a lifelong commitment. Because these years will be filled with pressures to "do it" and to fall for society's false promises, you must strive to focus on the gift and value of your sexuality and not be willing just to "give it away."

The challenge for you right now is to learn how to get along with other people, especially those of the other gender. Take the time to understand their feelings, thoughts, and dreams. What's their view on certain topics? What's important to them? How can you talk to them so that they understand what you really mean and feel? How can you listen better in order to understand their thoughts and feelings? These insights are important as you continue to learn how to be a true friend.

A stereotypical society

As you learn to understand persons of the other gender, you often need to go beyond the expectations society has placed on each gender. Under the headings below, list personality characteristics that you feel society expects of men and women.

Men are expected to be . . .   **Women are expected to be . . .**

Discuss the following questions with your class.
1. How can you look beyond these expectations?
2. How would our world be different if these expectations didn't exist?
3. How do you think our world needs to change some of these expectations?

It takes a lot of maturity and a lot of experience to learn how to be an unselfish, self-disciplined friend. It takes a lot of work to become a caring, sensitive, generous person. Yet these are the qualities you'll need before you're ready to make a lifetime commitment. By learning to be a true friend, you maintain the trust God has placed in you. These qualities will help you keep your sexual desires in control. Although this may seem tough at times, given human weakness in the face of temptation, God believes in your ability to treasure the value of your sexuality.

What does our culture teach?

It isn't hard to see that there are people in our culture who don't place much value on the gift of sexuality. Rather, they place much more importance on making money and creating pleasure, not on commitment within marriage. The emphasis is on recreation, with no thought of the power of creating human life. In fact, many aspects of our culture attempt to make you believe that the one thing to avoid at all costs is the creation of a new human life. Once you understand the value of your own sexuality, it is easier to see through the "myths" that are often presented as the "truths" about sexual relations.

Fact or fiction?

Take a close look at what the media presents as the norms for sexuality. For each of the following categories, list one example of a movie, magazine, and television series that presents a false view of the value of sexuality. Share your examples with the class.

• Movie:

• Magazine:

• Television series:

Discuss the following questions in a small group.

1. What are some ways in which you feel these types of media could present more accurate views of the value of sexuality?

2. Name some movies, magazines, and television series that you feel have attempted to present sexuality from a Christian viewpoint.

3. What would have to happen for our society to focus more on the value of sexuality than on the value of making money?

 What's your view?

Choose one song that you feel presents a wrongful view of sexuality. Write a portion of the lyrics below.

Now rewrite the lyrics from a Christian perspective.

Being sexually responsible

Your teenage years challenge you to be sexually responsible. Because many elements in our culture try to counteract what you know is right and try to undermine the value of sexuality, you must stay strong in your beliefs. All people are called to live a chaste life. Chastity requires that we remain pure in thought and action and that we maintain control over our sexual desires.

 Scripture Search

Jesus challenges us to live lives that are holy. Read 1 Thessalonians 4:2–8 and answer the following questions.

1. As disciples of Jesus, what are we instructed to do?

2. How can you best achieve this objective?

To stick to your beliefs and values, you first need to remember that you are somebody. You are capable of standing up for what is right. You can see through the myths and half-truths that are bombarding you from every direction—TV, movies, music, advertising, magazines, etc. If you stand strong in your belief that sexuality is for creation within the commitment of marriage, then you will not be easily brainwashed by the false idea that sexuality is simply a recreational activity. Remember, the gift of your sexuality is unique. Keeping yourself focused on this will help you be sexually responsible.

Second, you are in control of your sexual desires. Others may try to convince you that "everybody's doing it," but this is not true. Millions of teenagers are choosing not to be sexually active until marriage. So "everybody" often refers to the youth who have never learned the value of their sexuality. You are a somebody, a person capable of saving sex until you have made a lifelong commitment to someone. Waiting until marriage is both possible and responsible.

Spreading the word

Recently, there has been a strong push for abstinence among teens. Slogans such as "Virgin is not a dirty word" and "True love waits" are being seen on billboards across the United States. Below, create your own billboard idea that promotes the value of sexuality.

What difficulties do teenagers face when attempting to be sexually responsible in the way God calls us to be? List some ways that teens can ease these pressures.

_____

_____

_____

_____

The challenges you face

Your sexuality is a wonderful, awesome, life-giving gift. Even though God trusts you now with this powerful gift, it is intended to be used within the permanent and total friendship of marriage.

Many segments of our culture present an entirely different set of messages: Sex is for fun, recreation, and pleasure. As a responsible, young Christian, you are able to see through these myths and know that your sexuality holds great value.

Your real "sex education" right now needs to focus on understanding yourself and persons of the other gender and on

following the commandments and the teachings of the Church. Learning how to communicate, care, and show concern and respect for others is one of the many challenges you face during these years. By doing so, you also continue to learn about yourself. God believes in your ability to do this!

 THE NOTED QUOTED

"It is mutual respect which makes friendship lasting."

—John Henry Newman

⚜ Scripture Search

...do you not know that your body is a temple of the Holy Spirit within you, which you have from God, and that you are not your own? For you were bought with a price; therefore glorify God in your body.

—*1 Corinthians 6:19–20*

1. To what is your body compared?

2. What does it mean to "glorify God in your body"?

3. How can you teach this message to your peers?

Reflection

Reader #1: "So God created humankind in his image, in the image of God he created them; male and female he created them. God blessed them, and God said to them, 'Be fruitful and multiply, and fill the earth and subdue it; and have dominion over the fish of the sea and over the birds of the air and over every living thing that moves upon the earth.' God saw everything that he had made, and indeed, it was very good." (Genesis 1:27–28, 31)

Reader #2: Jesus, help me understand the powerful gift of my sexuality.

Reader #3: Give me the courage to see through popular myths about sexuality and to do what I know is right.

Reader #4: Give me the strength to be sexually responsible.

Reader #5: Teach me to be a true friend.

Reader #6: Help me wait until marriage to give the gift of my sexuality to another person.

All: Amen.

HOMEWORK

One of your friends has been dating someone for several months. He or she is being pressured to have sex. Write your friend a letter about the importance of saying "no" and what it means to be sexually responsible.

Dear

Your friend,

Chapter 6
Making Positive Choices
"Just Say No"

Nancy Reagan began the "Just Say No" anti-drug campaign in the 1980s during her husband's presidency. In the space below, list three other anti-drug and anti-alcohol slogans that promote responsible behavior among teenagers.

Share your slogans with the class and then discuss the following questions.

1. Which slogan do you feel is the most effective?

2. Which slogan do you feel teens "tune out" the most? Why is this slogan ineffective?

In a small group, create your own slogan promoting positive choices. Write your idea in the bumper sticker below.

I feel many teens start using drugs because:

_____

_____

_____

The choice is yours

It is often said that "a healthy mind requires a healthy body." The truth of this statement rings clear in regard to the use of alcohol and drugs. Today, the single greatest danger to both your mind and your body is drugs, which includes alcohol. In fact, alcohol is the number one most commonly used drug among teens. The harmful effects of drugs are numerous. You've heard about the dangers of crack, inhalants, marijuana, cocaine, heroin, hallucinogens, and alcohol. You'll continue to learn more information about the dangers of drug and alcohol use throughout high school.

The sad fact is that many youth choose to use and abuse drugs even though they know the dangers involved. It seems that just getting the information isn't enough. Thus, this chapter has a slightly different focus. It will look at why teens continue to use and abuse drugs despite all the warnings. Knowing these reasons may help you avoid making poor choices.

 THE NOTED QUOTED

"The strongest principle of growth lies in human choice."

—George Eliot

 Catechism Clip

The *use of drugs* inflicts very grave damage on human health and life. Their use, except on strictly therapeutic grounds, is a grave offense. Clandestine production of and trafficking in drugs are scandalous practices. They constitute direct co-operation in evil, since they encourage people to practices gravely contrary to the moral law. (2291)

Whom do you believe?

Perhaps one reason teenagers use drugs, especially alcohol, is that they simply don't take the warnings seriously, which is easy to understand. Millions of dollars are spent each year on advertising that tries to convince you of the joys and pleasures of drinking this beer or that wine cooler. Big-name celebrities are paid thousands of dollars to promote alcoholic products.

We hear of presidential candidates and political leaders who admit to previous or current drug use. Millionaire musicians sing about the pleasures of using this drug or popping that pill. Even many concerned parents unintentionally send out mixed messages by their own habitual use or abuse of alcohol or prescription drugs.

R.I.P.

List five famous persons you know who have lost their lives to alcohol and drug abuse.

1. What do their deaths teach young people today?

2. Why do you think so many famous people have died from drug overdoses?

3. What do you think can be done to change society's attitude regarding drugs and alcohol?

It's hard to take the warnings about the dangers of drugs seriously, especially regarding alcohol, when there are numerous messages saying drugs are the way many adults relax and have fun. So one of the main reasons all the information and warnings aren't enough to prevent drug abuse is simply because many youth don't believe what they're being told.

Another reason for drug abuse, similar to the first one, is the tendency many people have to believe that "It won't happen to me. Drug addiction, death by overdose, alcoholism, permanent brain damage—that all happens to other people. I'm different! I can handle it!" Most likely, every teenage and adult alcoholic or addict started out by thinking "It won't happen to me."

What about you? Whom do you believe? Do you believe the people and the studies that warn about the dangers of drugs? Do you believe the advertisements and song lyrics? Do you believe "It won't happen to me"? The choice is yours. But remember, your life depends upon how you answer these questions.

Write a short prayer of petition asking God to help you make positive choices regarding drugs and alcohol.

_____

_____

🦉 THE NOTED QUOTED

"If you don't stand for something, you'll fall for everything."

—Erikson

Why do teens start using?

All drugs, from a wine cooler to crack cocaine, produce an initial mind-altering effect called a "high." This "high" can be very appealing because it produces a quick way to escape problems and to feel good. Many teens want to find out what this "high" actually feels like, "just this once."

Curiosity, a desire to experiment "just this once," is a major reason many youth try drugs or alcohol. Despite all the warnings, they feel that experimenting "just once" cannot harm them. Yet no addict ever began with the goal of becoming an addict; no one expects to become addicted. Instead, many addicts began with the attitude of trying something new "just this once."

Together with curiosity, many times another force is at work. A peer or someone older is pressuring the youth. Sometimes the invitation seems harmless: "Try it. You'll like it." Other times the pressure can be strong: "Come on, you're not a baby anymore." "Look around, you're the only one not doing it."

How do you deal with negative peer pressure regarding drugs and alcohol?

_____

_____

In summary, the path of continued alcohol or drug use often begins with one of the following:

- curiosity
- the intention to try it "just this once"
- the idea that "it won't happen to me"
- a peer or group's pressure to try it

You may have already experienced some or all of these situations. Were you able to walk away? Were you strong in your beliefs? What will you do the next time you face a similar situation? It is up to you to make positive choices.

The great escape

Many people become almost instantly hooked on the ability of drugs to provide a "great escape." You see, most drugs have a mind-altering and mood-changing effect, sometimes occurring within minutes. They take away feelings such as shyness and fear. They help people forget their worries and problems, their weaknesses and failures. Most drugs create a temporary "make-believe" world, a world where everything seems perfect—especially the user.

That's what gets many youth hooked. They find that alcohol and other drugs provide a great escape from whatever it is they want to run away from. Usually, what they are trying to escape from is themselves. For a short time, they can escape into this "make-believe" world where they feel like a somebody.

It seems the youth who feel they are "nobodies" are often the ones most likely to get hooked on drugs. For a short while, at least, they can feel important, brave, fun to be with, good looking, or whatever it is they feel they aren't. You probably already know some peers who need to get "high" or escape from reality before they can have a good time.

Unfortunately, this "high" wears off. The user lands back in reality, often with a real "crash." As the effect of the drug wears off, there are usually some unpleasant physical side effects, such as a hangover, upset stomach, or severe headache.

 ## Scripture Search

Wine is a mocker, strong drink a brawler,
and whoever is led astray by it is not wise.

—*Proverbs 20:1*

1. What type of people are considered wise?

2. How can you be this type of person?

Even worse than the side effects is the mental or emotional "crash" that occurs afterward. Although it varies depending upon the drug, in almost every case the depression following a "high" is worse than the depression beforehand. Oftentimes the user is irrational, confused, fearful, or unable to keep his or her mind focused. If a person started out feeling like a nobody before the "great escape," during the "crash" afterward he or she will often feel even less self-worth.

Often the depression resulting from the "crash" lifts, but the old problems and the feelings of being a "nobody" are still there—maybe even worse than before. Suddenly the thought of "getting high" again looks very attractive. The thought of feeling like a somebody or escaping a problem seems like a good idea again. And it is so easy! That is often what happens. The person will drink this or smoke that "just one more time" to escape, and then

"one more time" after that. Before long, the person is hooked. He or she can no longer escape from the "great escape."

What's your view?

"Nobody is wise enough, nobody is good enough, and nobody cares enough for you to turn over to them your future and your destiny."

—*Dr. Benjamin Mays*

1. What does this quote say to you about the use of alcohol and drugs?

2. What plans do you have for your future that you won't allow drug use to take away?

Choosing alternate escape routes

When you are worried about a certain problem, the "great escape" can seem so appealing. The temptation to drink or to use other drugs can be very strong. But the quick fix doesn't really solve anything; more likely, it will add to the problem. Considering the risks and warnings connected to using alcohol or drugs, it seems smarter to start looking for alternatives, more permanent escape routes.

The good news is that there are plenty of alternatives available for teenagers today.

Usually the alternatives require that you identify your problem, fear, or worry and then meet it head-on rather than run from it. Once you've accepted that you want to live according to Jesus' example, you can start looking for the kind of help you really need to remedy the situation. You won't look to solve your problems with a bottle or with another form of a quick fix. You will look first to the Holy Spirit for guidance and strength. This in turn will lead you to prayer and the sacraments.

THE DOCTOR IS IN

When dealing with a problem, fear, or worry, it is best to create positive solutions. For each of the following situations, list positive ways in which a teenager could deal with the problem. Then think of five other "trouble" areas for teens and create possible solutions for each one.

1. If you are feeling shy, you could . . .

2. If you're feeling stressed from too much schoolwork, you could . . .

3. If you feel you don't "fit in" at your school, you could . . .

4.

5.

6.

7.

8.

You will find it easier to choose alternate activities that will help you become a better person and not someone needing a quick fix for your problems. If you avoid the problems of drinking and drugs in your teen years, you are much more likely to escape the problems forever.

Fun and Festivity

Many young people complain that there's nothing to do in their town or city. In actuality, the possibilities are as endless as your imagination. Using a phone book, a local newspaper, and your own creativity, list as many activities as you can for each of the four seasons.

If you feel you are trying to escape from negative feelings about yourself, you must first recognize the problem. By doing this, you take the first steps toward seeing yourself as a somebody. Then share your feelings with someone you trust—your mom or dad, a teacher or coach, a close friend, a priest or other parish minister, an older brother or sister. Together you can begin to focus on your positive talents and characteristics.

In any case, when you have a problem or worry, be smart enough to avoid the trap of dealing with it by using the "great escape" route. It leads to a dead end from which you may never be able to escape. Instead, use the guidance of the Church to create an alternate route that helps you deal with your problem head-on and in a positive way.

Many times, the best way to overcome a problem is by talking to another person. If you needed to talk to a trusted adult, who would be your first choice? Why?

_____

_____

_____

Show you care

Loyalty among your friends is very important. You want to know you can trust your friends with your innermost thoughts, feelings, and secrets. Yet if you have a friend who you know is continually using drugs or alcohol, being a loyal friend means trying to get help. This may mean confiding in a counselor, your friend's parents, or another adult. Hopefully, this person will have the power to get your friend the kind of assistance he or she needs.

It may seem that you're betraying your friend's trust, but in actuality, you are trying to save your friend's life. So when you really care for a friend and want to be loyal, telling someone else may be the only choice you have. With time, your friend will be glad you did!

THE NOTED QUOTED

"A friend in need is a friend indeed."
—English proverb

To whom can you turn?

When someone you know has turned to drugs or alcohol, it is important to know where you, as a friend, can go for help. Using a phone book, a local newspaper, or other resources, locate the telephone numbers for the following organizations that offer support and assistance to people whose lives are affected by drugs and alcohol. Add any information for additional support groups that you find.

- Alcoholics Anonymous:

- Narcotics Anonymous:

- Al-Anon:

- Alateen:

- Others:

Now turn to page 103 in the appendix of this text. Fill in the cards with the appropriate telephone numbers, cut them out, and keep them someplace handy. Then if someone you know ever needs help, give the appropriate card to your friend as a sign of your love and concern.

The right choice for life

As a young adult, you will be faced with many challenges regarding the use of drugs and alcohol, putting you in a "high risk" category. However, you have some advantages over many of your peers—you have the knowledge necessary to avoid the dangers of drugs and alcohol. It's important to know the hazardous effects drugs can have on your mind and body. Just as important, though, is knowing the reasons teens choose to use drugs despite the many warnings. If you understand the reasons, you are much more likely to make positive choices for your own life. You also have the guidance of the Church and God's grace to help you make the right decisions.

You know what lures teens into using drugs—the curiosity, the idea that they will experiment "just this once," and the false belief that "it won't happen to me." Many youth think that drinking or using other drugs can provide a "great escape" from their troubles. Knowing why teens begin to use drugs and alcohol can help you avoid these same traps. You'll recognize, if you haven't already, that every choice has consequences. If you always try to do good and avoid evil, what you learn through experience will be more than trial and error.

You know there are alternate routes to escape problems, including facing your troubles head-on and finding long-term solutions. You are a unique somebody who doesn't need alcohol or drugs to make you feel better about yourself. You are capable of making the right choice.

 ## Scripture Search

God has given you the power of choice. Read Deuteronomy 30:19–20 and answer the following questions.

1. When discussing drug and alcohol use and abuse, what would you consider "choosing life" to be?

2. What would it mean to "choose death"?

3. List some situations in which teens are faced with the decision to choose "life or death."

Reflection

Leader: Together let us pray.

All: Lord, help us make positive choices for our lives.

Help us be strong enough to say "no" to using alcohol and drugs as an escape from our problems.

Help us reach out to others who are using the "great escape." With your guidance, may we find other ways for them to deal with their problems.

Lord, help me be a good role model for those younger than me.

Amen.

HOMEWORK

What would you do to prevent drug and alcohol use among young people?

1. Three things I would teach young people:

2. Three rules I think every family should follow:

3. Three things schools can do to help:

4. Three things the Church can do to help:

5. Three things I would change in the way these problems are dealt with now:

6. How I would deal with:

   • pushers:

   • young people who are experimenting:

   • young people who are addicted:

7. If a close friend or a brother or sister started using drugs or alcohol,

   • I would tell him or her:

   • I would also:

Chapter 7
Learning To Act Justly
Think about It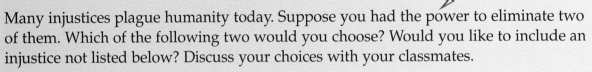

Many injustices plague humanity today. Suppose you had the power to eliminate two of them. Which of the following two would you choose? Would you like to include an injustice not listed below? Discuss your choices with your classmates.

War

Homelessness

Hunger

Racism

Violent Crime

Other: _____

Let's be fair

It's the day of the big math test. Before passing out the test, your math teacher announces that all those sitting in the first three rows can use calculators. Those sitting in the other rows, however, must take the test without calculators. You're in the last row and can't use the calculator. How do you feel?

Now imagine that you are in one of the rows that is allowed to use a calculator. You may share your calculator with a classmate that doesn't have one. It's up to you to decide. What would you do?

These imaginary situations represent situations of justice. The examples point out two main ideas: Justice is about fairness, and justice often requires sharing. The idea is simple enough, and yet so

many injustices continue to exist in our world: prejudice, discrimination, poverty, hunger, homelessness, disease, violence, abortion, destruction of the environment. Why is this? What can you do, as a disciple, to combat these injustices?

✂ Catechism Clip

Justice is the moral virtue that consists in the constant and firm will to give their due to God and neighbor. Justice toward God is called the "virtue of religion." Justice toward men disposes one to respect the rights of each and to establish in human relationships the harmony that promotes equity with regard to persons and to the common good. . . . (1807)

God asks us as disciples to be the workers for justice. We are called to use our gifts and talents to reach out to those in need. In order to do this, we must first recognize that all people are deserving of dignity and of having their basic needs met. This includes you, your friends, your family, the homeless person who lives downtown, your neighbor living with AIDS, the unborn child. Justice shall be served when all choose to live the Great Commandment, "You shall love your neighbor as yourself." For you as a disciple, this is and will be a challenge.

Think about It

Father Flanagan, the founder of Boys Town, told how one night a young boy showed up carrying on his back a smaller boy who was asleep. Father Flanagan said, "You must be tired from carrying that boy." The youth replied, "He's not heavy, Father. He's my brother."

We are called to consider everyone our brothers and sisters. What are some groups of people you would probably find it easy to consider as your brothers and sisters? Whom would you find it difficult to consider as your brothers and sisters?

_____
_____
_____
_____
_____
_____
_____
_____
_____
_____
_____
_____
_____

Some good news

The kingdom of God is God's reign of perfect peace, love, and justice. Although God's kingdom "is not from this world" (John 18:36) and will be fully realized only at the second coming, we work with God's kingdom whenever we follow the words and example of Jesus. The evening news is filled with acts of injustice, but for every sensational unjust act, there are many unseen, courageous, and wonderful just acts. For example, people in the United States tend to be very generous. They give millions of dollars each year to support hundreds of nonprofit organizations. Our country gives very generously through governmental and nongovernmental organizations each year to bring relief to victims of famine, war, and natural disasters around the world.

On the international level, people around the world are seeking justice. Many nations, not just our own, regularly send food, medicine, and other supplies to countries suffering from famine, war, and other disasters. There are many international organizations committed to helping children, to establishing peace, to assisting the poor, and to protecting the rights of the oppressed.

Surely his salvation is at hand for those who fear him,
  that his glory may dwell in our land.
Steadfast love and faithfulness will meet;
righteousness and peace will kiss each other.
Faithfulness will spring up from the ground,
  and righteousness will look down from the sky.

The LORD will give what is good,
  and our land will yield its increase.
Righteousness will go before him,
  and will make a path for his steps.
  —*Psalm 85:9-14*

And, of course, there is our Church. From its first days, the community of disciples established by Jesus has worked with God's kingdom of peace and justice by following the words and example of Jesus. Often the Church has been the leader, the first to speak out against injustice and the first to come to the aid of the poor and oppressed. As an institution made up of people, it has had its share of faults over the past two thousand years. But when you look at the whole picture, it is clear the Church is one of God's primary and most successful instruments for promoting the justice of God's kingdom. You are being called as a disciple of Jesus to join in this challenge to work with God's kingdom. This is a call to individuals to act and serve together by following the words and example of Jesus.

A kingdom of peace, love, and justice

Can you identify any of the following organizations in which people participate?

_____ Amnesty International	A. Human rights organization that encourages letter writing to help prisoners of conscience
_____ Bread for the World	B. Helps low-income families build and then own their own homes
_____ Catholic Relief Services	C. Operation Rice Bowl during Lent
_____ Church World Service	D. CROP walk for hunger
_____ Greenpeace	E. Christian citizens' movement devoted to influencing U.S. government policies on hunger
_____ Habitat for Humanity	F. Trick-or-treat for United Nations Children's Fund; also greeting cards
_____ Oxfam America	G. Fast for a World Harvest
_____ Pax Christi	H. Works on environmental issues
_____ Right to Life	I. Speaks out for the unborn
_____ UNICEF	J. Strives to create a world that reflects the Peace of Christ by exploring and witnessing to the call of Christian nonviolence

Understanding the problem

Write down what you think are five main reasons for the injustices in our history and why they continue today. Discuss.

1.

2.

3.

4.

5.

One of the reasons might be *selfishness.* Some people simply refuse to share. They choose to hang on to and enjoy their wealth, their power, their gifts and talents. They don't care about what happens to others, and they see no problem in treating others as objects to be used and abused for their own selfish purposes.

 THE NOTED QUOTED

Justice and power must be brought together, so that whatever is just may be powerful, and whatever is powerful may be just.

—Blaise Pascal

Another reason might be *fear.* Some people are concerned about the victims of injustice, but they are afraid to take the risks involved in helping them. They worry about sharing their goods because they might not have enough for themselves and their family. They may fear losing their rights when standing up for others.

Individualists tend to think that people with problems should be able to help themselves. They say things like "Poor people are just lazy" or "I've worked hard for what I have. Nobody helped me. The poor could do the same if they really wanted to. It's not my problem, and I don't owe them anything." Individualists think about themselves first. Sadly, individualism is abundant in the United States.

THE NOTED QUOTED

It is tempting at one level to believe that bad things happen to people (especially other people) because God is a righteous judge who gives them exactly what they deserve. By believing this we keep the world orderly and understandable. . . . But [this belief] has a number of serious limitations. . . . It teaches people to blame themselves. It creates guilt when there is no basis for guilt. It makes people hate God, even as it makes them hate themselves. And most disturbing of all, it does not even fit the facts.

—Harold S. Kushner, *When Bad Things Happen to Good People*

Many people are simply unaware of the injustice in society. They live their lives never noticing the pain and suffering around them. They are so busy that they never take time to recognize how much society needs them. These people may be willing to act, but they don't have the information and aren't looking for it.

Cynicism, *escapism*, and *helplessness* also affect people's willingness to act justly.

- Cynics say that it's impossible to do anything about injustice. Injustice has always been and always will be. All efforts to achieve justice are doomed to failure from the start. This attitude gives reason for not acting against injustice.

- Escapism lets a person stay busy and focused on his or her own interests in order to avoid facing the problems of injustice in the first place. People allow themselves to be so distracted by school, sports, social life, and entertainment that they never have to think about their responsibility to counter injustice. Escapism relates to both selfishness and individualism.

- Helplessness is a fairly common attitude among young people. Many adolescents say they are just one person and don't have any real influence, like adults do. They tell themselves they don't have the necessary talents. So even though they want to change things, there is really nothing they can do that would make a difference.

There is just enough truth in each of these attitudes to make them believable. That's why they are traps. So be on your guard. On the positive side, we have Jesus' promise that God's reign of peace, love, and justice will ultimately win out, no matter how bad things have been or still seem to be. It begins with an inner attitude filled with hope, respect, and compassion!

Justice is . . .

Use the letters in the word justice to begin a word or phrase that describes what justice involves.

J _____

U _____

S _____

T _____

I _____

C _____

E _____

You must have hope

Hope is perhaps the most fundamental attitude you, as a follower of Jesus, should have. Hope means you are convinced in your heart that God will always help, that good is going to overcome evil, and that God can and will establish his reign of justice and peace. Being effective at working for justice begins with being filled with hope that unjust situations can change and that one person can make a big difference. Rosa Parks, for example, refused to give up her seat on the bus to a white person in Montgomery, Alabama. Her refusal to accept the then-acceptable racist segregation encouraged one of the biggest civil rights movements in our country.

Working for justice involves some real risks. You risk ridicule and teasing; you risk the pain of failure; and sometimes you have to face the risk of physical harm. Hope gives you the courage to take these risks. The struggle for justice is a long-term struggle, but hope brings patience and perseverance, the "hang in there" attitude. People with hope are never quitters, no matter how bad things sometimes seem. Jesus hanging on the cross is the ultimate example of hope and the courage and patience that it gives.

 THE NOTED QUOTED

Christ has no body but yours. No hands, no feet on earth but yours. Yours are the eyes through which he looks with compassion on this world. Yours are the feet with which he walks to do good. Yours are the hands with which he blesses all the world.
—Saint Teresa of Avila

In the news

Cut five articles from the newspaper that deal with local, national, or international injustice in today's society. For each article, do the following:

• Name the injustice involved.

• Try to identify the cause.

• Suggest one thing that might be done to correct the problem.

Share your news articles and reports with the class or in small groups. These questions can help guide your sharing and discussion:

1. Did any of you choose some of the same articles?

2. What do you think is the greatest injustice found in all the articles? The most common injustice?

3. Do you agree or disagree on the kinds of causes given?

4. Discuss if any of the suggested solutions are actually workable.

5. Finally, discuss together and try to come to an agreement on the one most important thing you learned from this exercise. Write your conclusion here:

_____

_____

✂ *Catechism Clip*

Social justice can be obtained only in respecting the transcendent dignity of man. The person represents the ultimate end of society, which is ordered to him: "What is at stake is the dignity of the human person, whose defense and promotion have been entrusted to us by the Creator, and to whom the men and women at every moment of history are strictly and responsibly in debt." [John Paul II, *SRS* 47.] (1929)

Respect

We all tend to group people and to name them as a group; it is useful and necessary much of the time. For example, it makes more sense and is easier to say to a friend that the soccer team has practice on Saturday than it is to list the names of all the team members when sharing your news. We use numbers a lot, too, in describing people. Newspapers and newscasters do this all the time. You read statements like "One hundred people injured in train wreck" or hear news phrased "One thousand people lost their homes in the recent flood."

The fact is, of course, that every player on the soccer team *does* have a name, as do the one hundred people injured in the train wreck and the one thousand people who lost their homes. Individuals create our families, teams, communities, and news. Every individual is unique and precious. God considers each individual as a child deserving dignity and love. Each one of them is a special somebody.

Consider the terms we use when talking about people suffering from injustice: the poor, the unemployed, the homeless, the hungry. Now think of all the people those terms represent, each deserving the respect and the dignity of a child of God.

✂ Catechism Clip

There exist also sinful inequalities that affect millions of men and women. These are in open contradiction of the Gospel: "Their equal dignity as persons demands that we strive for fairer and more humane conditions. Excessive economic and social disparity between individuals and peoples of the one human race is a source of scandal and militates again social justice, equity, human dignity, as well as social and international peace. [*GS* 29 § 3.] (1938)

Thinking in terms of individual persons is a good foundation for social justice. Are you convinced that every person is worth caring for? Social justice requires that every person receives the dignity and respect they deserve, that we see everyone as our brother and sister. This profound respect for other persons, precisely as persons, calls us to action. In the work for social justice, this attitude and awareness has done more good in the world than anything else. What can you do to develop this attitude?

What's in a name?

When we use labels to describe people who are suffering injustices, we are not giving them the necessary respect and dignity each individual deserves. Choose one injustice that exists in our world today. Then write a fictional story about one person who suffers from that injustice. Think through what you believe their needs and feelings to be. Use your words to create the awareness that every person deserves the dignity and respect of others. Share your story with the class. If you are willing to, send the story to your local or diocesan paper for publication. Remember, one person can make a difference.

 THE NOTED QUOTED

Justice is achieved only when those who are not injured feel as angry as those who are.
—Plato

Be merciful, just as your Father is merciful. (Luke 6:36)

The third inner attitude necessary in our work for social justice lies in mercy, or compassion. To be compassionate is to feel another's pain. As a disciple, you must be willing to place yourself in the shoes of those who suffer. You must take time to know the pain of those who hurt because of injustice and then work to find ways to alleviate their pain. The gift of compassion calls you to step outside of your own world and to step into the world of injustice's victims. The Scriptures are filled with stories of how Jesus accomplished this. As a class, read together the following two stories centering on the compassion of Jesus: the story of Jesus feeding four thousand people (Matthew 15:32–38) and the story of the penitent woman (Luke 7:36–50).

When you see newscasts about the homeless or those living in poverty, take a moment to think about their situation. What would it be like to wake up and not have a roof over your head? What would you do if you had no idea where or what you would eat today? Having compassion allows you to understand the plight of another's life and to do what you can to alleviate suffering. This may happen on a large scale as you work to understand famine or on a local scale as you have compassion for someone being teased or cast out from the group. As a disciple of Jesus, you are called to follow in his footsteps of compassion for others.

Disciples of faith

See if you can recognize some people who display the qualities of justice.

_____ Harriet Tubman

_____ Martin Luther King Jr.

_____ Mahatma Gandhi

_____ Mother Teresa

_____ Nelson Mandela/Steven Biko

A. Worked with the poor in Calcutta, India

B. As leader of the Underground Railroad, this person worked to help free the slaves in the South

C. Chose nonviolence as means to gain Indian independence from Great Britain

D. Civil rights leader in the '60s

E. Fought the apartheid system in South Africa

Scripture Search

Read Mark 8:1–9 and write a short summary of what you think this passage means.

_____

_____

_____

_____

_____

Based on local, national, or international injustices, list three groups of people for whom you feel sad. Then try to name one practical thing this compassion moves you to do to help them.

1. _____

2. _____

3. _____

Compose a short prayer asking Jesus to help you develop the same kind of compassion he had.

_____

_____

_____

_____

Methods of action

Let's suppose you know and practice those basic inner attitudes of hope, respect, and compassion needed to bring about a more just society. How do you actually go about doing this? The following story might help answer this question.

A woman arrived at an area of town where there were many hungry people. She saw the great need and wanted to address it immediately, so she gave a fish to each person she encountered. No one in that area went to bed hungry that night.

Another person went to a similar area of town. He decided to teach the people to fish so they could feed themselves. It took them a while to learn, but once they did learn, everyone ate and was satisfied.

Feed people fish and they'll eat for a day. Teach people to fish and they'll eat for a lifetime.

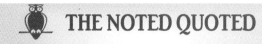

THE NOTED QUOTED

Justice is truth in action.
—Benjamin Disraeli

Effects or causes

The "immediate result" approach focused on the "here and now" effects that injustice has on people. If you meet a man on the street who is penniless, homeless, and hungry, giving him your sack lunch will relieve his immediate need to have something to eat. Likewise, soup kitchens, shelters, being friendly to those who are outcasts, and answering crisis line telephones all address the pain that is being felt now.

We also need the patience and perseverance to challenge the causes of injustice. Accepting delayed results allows us to affect the laws, institutional practices, overpopulation, and ignorance that result in poverty, racism, violence, etc. Educational programs on racism and violence, writing government officials and companies, recycling and purchasing recycled goods, and talking openly about topics such as sex and pregnancy may take a while to affect the problem, but they will eventually affect the cause of the problem.

You may decide to work for immediate or delayed results. Need is great for both types of action. Addressing the effects of injustice allows you to see the results of your work almost immediately. Accepting delayed results means that you address the causes of injustice. For example, the Missionaries of Charity, the order founded by the late Mother Teresa, address both the causes and the effects of injustice. They live among the poor and feed the hungry, clothe the naked, and care for the sick. They also speak out at public meetings against injustice and educate those who are ignorant of these injustices. Working together to fight both the causes and effects is the best way to eliminate injustice.

A Person of Note

Joan Holmes is the president of a group called *The Hunger Project: Unleashing the Human Spirit for the End of World Hunger*. She and her groups are very active in addressing hunger throughout the world. Their public statements and actions help curb both the causes and the effects of hunger.

Two goals that Joan Holmes suggests are:

1. Enable every child, woman, and man to meet their basic needs—access to good primary health care, a basic education, clean water, good nutrition, and safe sanitation.
2. Ensure that our natural environment is restored and preserved.

The Hunger Project feels that the challenges of hunger and poverty, health, and the environment are matters of life and death for millions of people. These issues are also the primary threat to security and peace for all, now and in the future. Furthermore, these are not separate issues and cannot be solved in isolation. What follows is a portion of Holmes's speech at the Second Global Youth Conference for the End of World Hunger in August 1995.

The Most Global Generation

I know that you have often heard people call you "the leaders of tomorrow." But I say: You are the leaders of today—the leaders who will enable humanity to have a tomorrow. You are uniquely prepared to take up this challenge. Your generation is global. You travel more. You share a world culture of music.

The communication revolution has linked you to your brothers and sisters around the world in ways previous generations could not have dreamed. Many of you have a mastery of computers—a level of empowerment with information undreamed of only a few decades ago.

The world needed a generation to be global—and created you.

A little bit means a lot

Whether you decide to address the effects or causes of injustice, always remember that every little bit helps. There are no small, unimportant acts when it comes to justice; success is measured one person at a time. Showing your sincere respect to a victim of prejudice won't make the six o'clock news, but it will make that one child of God sleep a little easier tonight. Giving a dollar to AIDS research may not seem like much, but without it, one less test is performed. Even if you start small, everything done for the sake of justice is very important.

As a disciple of Jesus, you can speak out against injustice when you see or hear it. You can challenge your friends and speak out against a prejudice in your school, for example. You can join with others in a public march to support life. You do not need to speak loudly or aggressively. In fact, speaking politely and respectfully may gain better results. You could, for example, quietly tell someone when others aren't around that you did not appreciate his or her joke about homosexuals, that it was insulting and not an appropriate subject matter for jokes. Such a "little bit" of speaking out can make a large difference.

 ## THE NOTED QUOTED

Grain by grain—a loaf. Stone by stone—a palace.
—Bulgarian proverb

 ## Getting Started

Let's get started. To speak out against injustice, you need to get to know and trust your own gifts. Choose from the following list the gifts or talents you think you have to share with others. Then draw a line to the area in which you think you might be able to use that gift to work for justice.

I am . . .

_____ a leader

_____ a good listener

_____ artistic

_____ a good cook

_____ a good card player

_____ musically-gifted

_____ athletic

_____ a hard worker

_____ other _____

1. Design flyers for fund-raisers to raise money for the needy
2. Walk/run to raise money for charity
3. Volunteer at a senior citizen center
4. Work at a soup kitchen
5. Volunteer at a hospital
6. Help with building low-income housing
7. Write a song to encourage people to become involved in helping others in some way
8. Organize an Amnesty International writing campaign
9. _____

Start locally

It is often best to focus on a local need, one that's right in your town, in your school, in your neighborhood, or even in your own home. Is there something you can do to make outcasts feel welcome in your school? Can you try to get your own family to do a better job of recycling? Does the parish food pantry need volunteers? Working with and for people you know may be a good place to start.

✂ *Catechism Clip*

"Participation" is the voluntary and generous engagement of a person in social interchange. It is necessary that all participate, each according to his position and role, in promoting the common good. This obligation is inherent in the dignity of the human person. (1913)

Get all the info

Become as informed as you can on the issue. A lot of people act purely on emotion. They don't take the time to learn the real causes of the problem and the realistic solutions. In a short time they experience difficulties, or their emotions die down, and they lose interest. If you want to work for justice, you have to commit your time and energy. So take the time to learn as much as you can about the problem. Be willing to become an "expert" on it and stay informed and involved.

Work together

Most problems of injustice have been around a long time, and there are all kinds of groups already working to overcome most of them. Joining a group is one of the quickest ways to learn about the problem—what the real causes are, what solutions have been tried in the past, what seems to work, what hasn't worked. Working with a group also has many other advantages—friendships, support, encouragement. It is especially important to work with a group when trying to achieve a delayed result. It's difficult to stay committed for a long-term cause, but it's easier when you work with others. Once you choose an area of injustice you'd like to address, check around for existing groups in your area that have your concern as their goal, too. You might start with your own parish.

🦉 THE NOTED QUOTED

If you want peace, work for justice.

—Pope Paul VI

✠ *More disciples of faith* ✠

Match each of the following individuals or groups with the issue for which they work or worked.

_____ 1. Rainforest Action Network   A. AIDS

_____ 2. Christopher Reeve   B. Poor in El Salvador

_____ 3. Arthur Ashe   C. Spinal injury research

_____ 4. Peace Troupe   D. Hunger

_____ 5. Joan Holmes   E. Political prisoners

_____ 6. Sting   F. Violence/aggression

_____ 7. Jean Donovan   G. Environment

Which groups or persons did you recognize. Did you know of their social justice works? Which of these issues interests you most? Which of your talents can contribute to these issues?

Wrap-up

Having the right attitudes of hope, respect, and compassion are critical to promoting social justice. You can work for immediate or delayed results. However you work, remember that every little bit helps. To get started in works of justice, there are four practical tips to follow: get to know your gifts, start locally, become informed, and work with others. With these tools, you can indeed act as a disciple of Jesus, working to challenge the injustices in our world today!

Reflection

You, and all disciples, are called to walk in the footsteps of Jesus. As a class, pray together *A Disciple's Way of the Cross*, which can be found in the appendix on pages 105–7. When finished, discuss with your class how you are called to walk similar steps of justice in your own lives.

HOMEWORK

A. Complete the following sentences by filling in the blanks with the correct word.

1. The attitude that helps you trust God and "hang in there" in the struggle to overcome injustice is _____.

2. _____ is the attitude that enables you to share in the suffering of the victims of injustice.

3. When you remember that every person is a special child of God, you develop the attitude of _____.

4. In working for immediate results, you try to relieve the _____ of injustice.

5. In working for delayed results, you try to address the _____ of injustice.

6. A _____ is someone willing to go public, speak out, and take a stand against injustice.

B. List the four tips for getting started in working for justice:

1. _____

2. _____

3. _____

4. _____

C. Identify a specific act of injustice present in your area and develop your own personal plan for promoting justice in this situation.

Chapter 8

Accepting Challenges

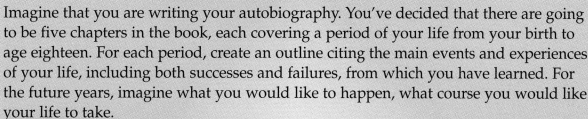

My Autobiography

Imagine that you are writing your autobiography. You've decided that there are going to be five chapters in the book, each covering a period of your life from your birth to age eighteen. For each period, create an outline citing the main events and experiences of your life, including both successes and failures, from which you have learned. For the future years, imagine what you would like to happen, what course you would like your life to take.

• Chapter 1: birth to age four

• Chapter 2: ages five to ten

• Chapter 3: ages eleven to fourteen

• Chapter 4: ages fifteen to sixteen

• Chapter 5: ages seventeen to eighteen

The story of your life

Growing up is much like writing your autobiography. The first few chapters are already written, of course. They are about your childhood, and they give some shape and direction to what is going to follow. But now you must write the rest of the story. How it turns out is up to you and God. No one can write this part of the story for you.

THE NOTED QUOTED

"There is no limit to the goals you can attain, the success you can achieve—your possibilities are as endless as your dreams."

—D. Crowe

Catechism Clip

Divine providence consists of the dispositions by which God guides all his creatures with wisdom and love to their ultimate end. (321)

Your main concern right now is for the upcoming chapters dealing with your teen years, the years "in between" childhood and adulthood. These chapters are very important right now. As you begin this section of your autobiography, you will find high school to be the setting for this part of your story.

This course has dealt with some of the challenges and tasks you'll face during this period. Topics such as continuing to believe in yourself, learning to communicate with your parents, and developing your prayer life, or faith dimension, were discussed to give you strength and guidance during these years. We've talked about the role friends and peers play, the need to deal with your sexuality in a responsible way, and the need to understand the risks of alcohol and other drugs.

Much of your autobiography will be filled with your successes, and sometimes failures, in each of these areas. Remember that personal happiness comes from rejoicing in your successes and learning from your failures.

Scripture Search

Read the Beatitudes in Matthew 5:2–12. Explain in your own words what these statements tell us about true blessedness.

_____
_____
_____
_____
_____
_____
_____

As you grow into adulthood, every one of your experiences will teach you something and, to a large degree, determine how you will live the remaining chapters of your story. Your challenge is to "write" the story of your life as well as you can, knowing that the ending is the beginning of forever.

If you were to publish your autobiography, to whom would you dedicate it? Why?

_____
_____
_____
_____
_____

THE NOTED QUOTED

"Two roads diverged in a wood, and I—I took the one less traveled by, and that has made all the difference."

—Robert Frost

Learning to use an eraser

If you want to get the most out of your "in-between" years, you need to realize that you cannot succeed or know what you're good at without trying new things. High school is the perfect time to do some "exploring." By exploring different hobbies, clubs, sports, and organizations, you have the opportunity to meet new people and expand your circle of friends.

Some things will work out and others won't. You may discover new talents, but at the same time, uncover weaknesses. You'll have successes and failures. You may even make some mistakes. That's okay—that's what erasers are for. If you want to write a successful autobiography, you'll have to do some erasing from time to time. But you'll also discover you've got skills and talents you never dreamed you had. Growing means taking some risks and being willing to explore what's

possible. It means doing some erasing and rewriting.

Although failures are not enjoyable or easy to face, they do help you discover your talents and your limits. They help you zero in on areas you may need to strengthen. Suppose, for example, you try out for the soccer team or audition for the school jazz band. You don't make it, but in the process, you uncover a weak spot that you can work to improve on the next time.

"Psst!
When opportunity knocks,
Don't pace the floor;
Grab the handle
and open the door!"

—*Joanne Bonwick*

Describe a time in your life when opportunity knocked and you answered the door.

_____

_____

_____

_____

_____

 **Scripture Search**

Read the story of the good Samaritan in Luke 10:25–37 and answer the following questions.

1. Which people in the story failed to do what was right?

2. What "success" in God's eyes does the good Samaritan achieve?

3. Describe some times in your life when you failed to act like the good Samaritan.

4. What are some times when you did act like the good Samaritan?

If your weak spot is something you can improve on, you must decide whether or not you want to work at it and sharpen your skills. If it's something all the practice in the world can't change, then you know it is time to start focusing on a new interest. You may decide to erase soccer or the jazz band from your autobiography. But remember this—there's a big difference between saying "I'm not good at soccer or playing jazz" and saying "I'm not good at anything." You are a somebody with many abilities and strengths. Keep writing and erasing and rewriting your autobiography until you find out just what your talents are.

 THE NOTED QUOTED

"Success is not the result of spontaneous combustion. You must set yourself on fire."
—Reggie Leach

Fearing everything, you will go nowhere; but when you put your faith in God, you can get anywhere.
—*Erin McGarry, age 15*

Describe some times in your life when you need to place your faith in God in order to accomplish what it is you want to do.

_____
_____
_____
_____
_____
_____
_____
_____

The power of forgiveness

Just as being willing to ask for advice or help is a sign of maturity and intelligence, so is being able to ask for forgiveness. In the coming years, you will make mistakes. It's part of the human condition because of the consequences of original sin and because of our misuse of free will, part of growing up, part of life. That is why it is so important to keep in mind that God forgives you when you ask for forgiveness. God is always ready to forgive. Jesus wants you as his disciple, a disciple who is happy and enjoys life. Jesus knows and understands the challenges you face.

 THE NOTED QUOTED

"It is a struggle to climb a mountain, but the view from the top is magnificent."

—John Powell

God is ready and eager to forgive, to forget, and to help you start over, no matter how often you may fall into sin or make mistakes. The eraser God uses is the most powerful eraser in existence. It's called mercy. Catholics celebrate this mercy in the Sacrament of Reconciliation. In this sacrament, we repent, admit our sinfulness, and promise to change our harmful habits. God forgives us and graces us with the strength to begin again.

God doesn't want you to fail, but he understands when you do. So don't get discouraged with yourself. In the eyes of God, you will always be a unique, special somebody. Admitting your mistakes, being sorry, and asking for help is the way to deal with any sinfulness you experience. You erase it from your story with God's help and start writing again.

 THE NOTED QUOTED

"Never let the fear of striking out keep you from swinging."

—Babe Ruth

You also need to learn how to forgive yourself. Mistakes, major failures, and sins that you know are your fault do not keep you from being the unique, special somebody you are. What they do tell you is that you are a somebody who has some more work to do on your autobiography in order to get it right.

The autobiography of our Church

There is also the challenge to understand the story of the Church. Like you, the Catholic Church has grown and changed and will continue to do so. Yet it remains rooted in the teachings of Jesus and finds guidance in the Spirit. God invites you to be part of the Church because he knows you are capable of carrying on Jesus' message and actions. God sees talents and abilities in you that you don't yet see in yourself. You are part of God's plan. In a real sense, God needs you as a disciple in our world today.

In order to be a better disciple, it is necessary to understand how the Church is organized and how it operates. The Church has many sides and perspectives to it. There are many images and figures of speech used to explain the Church, such as Jesus' image of the Church as living branches attached to him, the life-giving vine, or Saint Paul's use of the image of the body, with Christ as our head and all of us as different parts. Each description gives us a slightly different aspect of looking at this mystery called Church. To limit our image of Church to just one description narrows the larger picture of Church.

✂ Catechism Clip

The Church is the Body of Christ. Through the Spirit and his action in the sacraments, above all the Eucharist, Christ, who once was dead and is now risen, establishes the community of believers as his own Body. (805)

The following diagram offers six models to describe our Church. Each model offers a unique view of how the Church carries out its mission. By looking at each model separately, you can broaden your understanding of the many components of our Church.

At the center

Notice that Jesus and the Spirit are at the center of the diagram. They are the source and the life force that keep the Church together and alive. The Church takes its nature and its mission from Jesus and continues to guide disciples through the Spirit in this mission. The Church exists to carry on Jesus' mission of announcing and helping create God's reign among us. The Church is the extension of Jesus through history. This is made possible because our Church has remained centered on the teachings of Jesus and the guidance of the Spirit.

 ## THE NOTED QUOTED

"I never saw him. I never heard him. I never touched him. But there were those who did. And they told others, who told others, who told others still, who eventually told me. And now, in my turn, I tell you so you too can tell others. And so, you see, there will never be an end to the life and message of Jesus."

—John Shea

Discipleship

As you spend time with Jesus, you'll be growing in your discipleship. Being a disciple begins inside yourself. It's a special way of relating to Jesus. It's saying yes to Jesus' invitation to be his friend and follower. Disciples are "best friends" with Jesus. Being community is another part of the challenge. It means "being family" with the other disciples of Jesus. This involves overcoming a big obstacle.

Many people consider their faith a private matter, something between themselves and God. However, we can't really be a community of disciples unless we're willing to share with one another about our common friendship with Jesus. How about yourself? Do you find it difficult and embarrassing to discuss your faith, your prayer life, your feelings about God, the problems you have following Jesus? Most teens do. Yet this sharing is exactly what a community of disciples has in common. We support and encourage each other through sharing and help each other grow. Learning to be open and willing to talk about your faith with other believers, especially those your own age, is one of the most important ways you'll come to understand what Church is all about.

The three Greek words, kerygma *(message),* koinonia *(community), and* diakonia *(service) are often used to describe the work of Jesus' disciples.*

Scripture Search

Jesus invited everyone into friendship with God. Read each of the following Scripture passages and match it with the person Jesus invited.

_____ 1. A woman caught in adultery	A. Matthew 8:1–4
_____ 2. A deaf man	B. Matthew 17:14–18
_____ 3. A boy with a demon	C. Mark 2:1–12
_____ 4. A criminal	D. Mark 7:31–35
_____ 5. A leper	E. Luke 18:35–43
_____ 6. A paralyzed man	F. Luke 19:1–10
_____ 7. A blind beggar	G. Luke 23:39–43
_____ 8. Zacchaeus the tax collector	H. John 8:1–11

School Days

Your school is an institution. Use specific examples from your school of three key parts of an institution to complete the following:

Common goals, values, truths, and ideals

Rules and recognized leaders

Key symbols, events, and heroes and heroines

Institution

A second model of the Church focuses on how the Church is organized on the outside. Like any institution, the Church needs to maintain order to be successful.

Because the Church is distinctive from other institutions, though, its key elements of order are distinctive, too. We call them creed, code, and cult.

 ## The Three "C"s of Our Church

Look up the definitions of creed, code, and cult in a dictionary. Although there may be several definitions listed for each word, write below the definition that pertains to the Church and our faith. Then use each word properly in a complete sentence.

• Creed

• Code

• Cult

Creed. The institution of Church has a common set of truths, ideals, goals, and values that all its members agree to and accept. These are summarized in the official teachings of the Church. As members of the Church, we are expected to know and accept this creed.

Code. The institution of Church has a common set of rules to follow: the Ten Commandments and the laws of the Church. Our code also includes guidelines to determine who our leaders are, how we settle disagreements, and the process for creating rules.

The laws that govern the institutional Church are called canons and are contained in the Code of Canon Law. *This Code has been revised periodically through the centuries.*

Cult. The institution of the Church has common symbols, rituals, special heroes and heroines, feast days and celebrations to remember and to keep alive our ideals, goals, and truths.

Without the creed, code, and cult, the community of disciples that Jesus formed may have ceased to exist soon after Jesus ascended to heaven. People naturally require structure to proceed with an idea beyond the first day. Imagine how important that is to an idea that is two thousand years old!

Teacher

A third model of Church centers on the challenge to all of us to be teachers. Jesus relayed his knowledge of God to his disciples, the Church. Thus, the Church was given the fullness of God's personal revelation (truth). This revelation enables the Church to teach about God. Following the example of Jesus, we are all called to teach what has been revealed about God.

Listen and Learn

During the liturgy, the homily is a time for the priest to teach the people about the message of Jesus. Choose one lesson from the Gospels. Below, explain the lesson and where you found it.

Now take some time (perhaps over a period of days) to prepare a homily. On a separate sheet of paper, write a brief explanation to help your peers live this gospel lesson in their daily lives.

As teacher, the Church's job is to proclaim, explain, and maintain the revelation God has entrusted to it. Today the Church needs the most help proclaiming the good news to others. This is one area to which you can contribute. As you proclaim your faith, you become more comfortable discussing your faith with others. There is so much good news to share about how Jesus brought us life through his death. And there are many people who haven't yet heard the news. Your challenge is to grow in willingness and courage to proclaim this good news. Sometimes you will use words. More often you will proclaim the news through your actions and attitude toward people!

Sacrament

A fourth model of Church is sacrament, the call to be a priestly people. As sharers in the priesthood of Christ, we are called to be a visible contact point between God and the world. Every member of the Church shares in this priestly mission. In addition to some men who are chosen to be ordained priests, we are *all* called to bring others to the faith. We become a visible sign of God's holiness and love when we worship, pray, care for the needy, love the outcasts, and defend the weak. We are asked to make "sacrifices" in our lives and to take time to make our lives holy. This is readily accomplished through prayer and the sacraments, especially the Eucharist.

✂ Catechism Clip

The whole Church is a priestly people. Through Baptism all the faithful share in the priesthood of Christ. This participation is called the "common priesthood of the faithful." Based on this common priesthood and ordered to its service, there exists another participation in the mission of Christ: the ministry conferred by the sacrament of Holy Orders, where the task is to serve in the name and in the person of Christ the Head in the midst of the community. (1591)

The entire Church, both ordained and lay people, has similar priestly tasks to do in and for the world. Like Jesus, all members of the Church must strive to gather people into the faith. We need to be a visible sign of God's love for others and to offer what we can to make the world holy for God.

Scripture Search

When Saint Paul left a community, he would choose someone to continue to be the official person around whom the faith community would gather. Review the following Scripture passages and then name the person Saint Paul appointed to this role.

• 1 Corinthians 16:15–16 _____

• Ephesians 6:21 _____

• Colossians 4:17 _____

Servant

The servant model of Church has a rather straight and simple lesson. As Church we share in Jesus' kingship. Unlike the kings we find in fairy tales, being a king like Jesus means being a shepherd, a servant, a footwasher, a host. Even the official authorities in the Church are servants and footwashers. Our kingship involves showing special attention to the people most in need of service or hospitality—the people society tends to overlook.

There is a little-known monument in Washington, D.C., near Saint Matthew's Cathedral, entitled "Nuns of the Battlefield." It honors the six hundred Catholic sisters who volunteered to serve as nurses immediately behind the battle lines during the Civil War.

 ## Scripture Search

To review how Jesus taught his apostles to be footwashers—servants—for others, read together as a class the story in John 13:1–17. What names do we use today for those who are footwashers or servants?

You can start by taking more notice of the blessings and gifts you have to share. Grateful people are the best givers. Remember the words Jesus spoke: The most talented, powerful, capable, and gifted should be the servants of those in need.

 ## Catechism Clip

. . . For the Christian, "to reign is to serve [Christ]," particularly when serving "the poor and the suffering, in whom the Church recognizes the image of her poor and suffering founder." [*LG* 8; cf. 36.] The People of God fulfills its royal dignity by a life in keeping with its vocation to serve with Christ. . . . (786)

Community of believers

The final model of Church is the community of believers. This model combines the other five models, remaining focused on Jesus and the Spirit at the center. As a community of believers, we are called to live a life of discipleship, to be part of an institution, to teach others, to act as a priestly people, and to serve those in need. The focus of the sixth model is how the Church can work together as Christians to perform these duties.

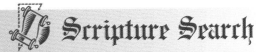

God has chosen you to be a member of the special group formed to bring the reign of God to the entire world. You've been called. You've been invited. Don't think you are too young to accept the invitation. David was about your age when God called him to be the king of Israel. Mary was about your age when she received her special invitation to be the mother of Jesus. Timothy felt he was too young to accept the invitation to the call. Read 1 Timothy 4:12 to discover what Paul said in his letter to Timothy. Write the verse below to inspire you when you also feel too young to follow Jesus.

As a disciple, you are a member of this community. You are called to be an active member of the Church. Your options for involvement are endless! Knowing these models of Church can help you focus on which areas you would like to be involved. Choose one or combine them all. Whatever your choice, always know that your work as a disciple is important to the life of the Church.

 Scripture Search

As you continue to be a disciple in the world today, you need to practice your virtues. Read Colossians 3:12–17.

1. List five virtues that as a disciple you need to have.

-
-
-
-
-

2. Why are these virtues necessary to be a disciple of Jesus?

Putting it all together

This course has been about discipleship. At times it probably didn't seem like it. Instead, it probably seemed to deal more with growing up, using commonsense ideas to handle the challenges you face, and gaining knowledge about the Church. The truth is this: Becoming a good disciple means that you believe in yourself, learn to relate to your parents, choose your friends wisely, grow continually in your faith, understand the value of your sexuality, make positive choices, learn to act justly, and accept challenges.

To be a disciple of Jesus, you don't have to do extraordinary things—just do the ordinary things well. Becoming fully human, discovering and believing you are a unique somebody, are the tasks you face every day as a disciple. You must work to accomplish them one day at a time.

 THE NOTED QUOTED

"The talent of success is nothing more than doing what you can do well and doing well whatever you do."

—Longfellow

 Scripture Search

The Scriptures often offer an image of what it means to be a disciple. Read 1 Corinthians 9:24–25 and answer the following questions.

1. What image is used to describe discipleship?

2. What does the "winner" receive?

3. Choose another image to describe discipleship. Describe your idea here.

You see, growing up and becoming a disciple takes place one day at a time, one decision at a time. Be patient with the process. Worrying about possible problems you may face next year keeps you from living today to its fullest. So does stewing about last week's mistakes. Focus on doing your best today!

 THE NOTED QUOTED

"Dare to dream—dare to try—dare to fail—dare to succeed."

—G. Kinsley Ward

God has given you all the gifts, talents, and intelligence you'll need to be the kind of *somebody* you are called to be. Develop your own gifts. Being jealous of what others seem to have keeps you from being your best self. Discover your own talents and then look for opportunities to share them with others.

In addition, God, a loving Father, has given you the Bible, the Church, and most of all, Christ, as a model and our Savior.

Now is the time to continue writing your autobiography, a page at a time, a day at a time. Include your successes and use your eraser for your failures. Add the stories that brought you joy, pain, humor, and tears. Incorporate your growing knowledge of faith and of the Church. All of your experiences are an important part of your story that can lead to a happy ending with God in eternity. Happy writing!

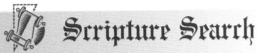
Scripture Search

Jesus looked at them and said, "For mortals it is impossible, but not for God; for God all things are possible."

—*Mark 10:27*

1. What are some of your dreams that you would like to make come true?

2. Which one of your talents would you like to improve even more?

3. Who is one person you believe has definitely made his or her dream come true? Tell this person's story.

Reflection

Leader: Jesus, you call all of us to be your disciples. Let us listen now to a story of the call of your first disciples from Luke 5:1–11.

Reader #1: Once while Jesus was standing beside the lake of Gennesaret, and the crowd was pressing in on him to hear the word of God, he saw two boats there at the shore of the lake; the fishermen had gone out of them and were washing their nets. He got into one of the boats, the one belonging to Simon, and asked him to put out a little way from the shore. Then he sat down and taught the crowds from the boat.

Reader #2: When he had finished speaking, he said to Simon, "Put out into the deep water and let down your nets for a catch."

Reader #3: Simon answered, "Master, we have worked all night long but have caught nothing. Yet if you say so, I will let down the nets." When they had done this, they caught so many fish that their nets were beginning to break. So they signaled their partners in the other boat to come and help them. And they came and filled both boats, so that they began to sink.

Reader #4: But when Simon Peter saw it, he fell down at Jesus' knees, saying, "Go away from me, Lord, for I am a sinful man!" For he and all who were with him were amazed at the catch of fish that they had taken; and so also were James and John, sons of Zebedee, who were partners with Simon.

Reader #5: Then Jesus said to Simon, "Do not be afraid; from now on you will be catching people." When they had brought their boats to shore, they left everything and followed him.

Reader #6: Jesus, thank you for calling each of us. Like Simon, James, and John, we accept the challenge to be your disciples.

Reader #7: Help us always to be open to advice and to ask questions to help us along the path we take.

Reader #8: Help us learn from our failures and focus on our successes.

Reader #9: Jesus, thank you for your friendship. We are ready to be your disciples in our world today.

All: Amen.

HOMEWORK

There are many challenges that go with being a disciple in today's world. Eight of these challenges were introduced and discussed in this course. Your job now is to make a plan on how you are going to meet these challenges in your own life. This plan is an important part of your autobiography and will add to the success of your life story.

1. **Believing in yourself:** Jesus' second great commandment is "You shall love your neighbor as yourself" (Matthew 22:39). In order to do this, we must first know how to love ourselves.

   • As a disciple, I plan to . . .

2. **Relating to your parents:** Your relationship with your parents or guardians is changing and growing. Your goal is to understand them better and relate to them.

   • As a disciple, I plan to . . .

3. **Choosing your friends:** It is important to choose your friends wisely and to know how to stand up against the harmful pressures of your peers.

   • As a disciple, I plan to . . .

4. **Growing in your faith:** As you grow physically, mentally, emotionally, and spiritually, you become aware of God's presence in your life and learn to take time for prayer and service.

   • As a disciple, I plan to . . .

5. **Understanding the value of sexuality:** God trusts you to use the gift of your sexuality in a mature and responsible way. Indeed, it is a precious gift to be treasured.

- As a disciple, I plan to . . .

6. **Making positive choices:** During this time in your life, it is likely that you will be faced with the choice of whether or not to use drugs, including alcohol. It is important for you to learn how to make positive choices.

- As a disciple, I plan to . . .

7. **Learning to act justly:** As you mature, you gain a desire to make the world a better place. You strive to meet the challenge to be a worker for justice, to reach out to those people in need.

- As a disciple, I plan to . . .

8. **Accepting challenges:** As you make decisions and take some risks, you will enjoy successes, overcome obstacles, and learn from failures.

- As a disciple, I plan to . . .

Appendix

YOU—A DISCIPLE!

Contract for Responsibilty

I, _____ , promise to be more responsible in my everyday actions.

I hereby promise to show my responsibility by

Please let me know how you think I am doing!

Thank you!

_____
Witness

_____
Signature

_____
Date

_____
Date

A Guide to the Bible

When you desire inner peace,
read John 14 or Romans 8.

When you feel lonely or fearful,
read Psalms 27, 91, Luke 8:1–16,
or 1 Peter 4:12–19.

When you feel everything is going well,
read Psalm 33:12–22, 1 Timothy 6:6–10,
or James 2:1–13.

When you feel your faith is weak,
read Psalms 126, 146, or Hebrews 11.

When you feel satisfied with yourself,
read Proverbs 11 or Luke 16:19–31.

When you have sinned,
read Psalm 51:1–12, Isaiah 53:1–5,
or John 3:1–21.

When you marvel at how you are made,
read Psalm 139.

When you want to know the way to pray,
read or Luke 11:1–13.

When you want to praise God,
read Daniel 3:59–90.

When you are discouraged,
read Psalms 23, 42, or 43.

When you think God seems far away,
read Psalms 25 and 138.

When you lose someone close to you,
read Colossians 1:24–29 or 1 Peter 1:3–12.

When you find life to be too busy,
read Ecclesiastes 3:1–15.

When you can't get to sleep,
read Psalms 4, 56, or 130.

When you are tired and weary,
read Matthew 11:28–30.

When you are jealous,
read Psalm 49 or James 3:1–12.

When you are worried,
read Psalm 46 or Matthew 6:25–34.

When you are facing a crisis,
read Proverbs 9 or Isaiah 55.

When you are in a quarrel,
read Matthew 18:15–35,
Ephesians 4:25–32, or James 4:1–12.

When you need forgiveness,
read Luke 15.

When you feel "blue,"
read Psalms 34 or Isaiah 40.

When you are sick or in pain,
read Psalms 6, 39, 41, or 67.

When you are tempted to do wrong,
read Psalm 15, Matthew 4:1–11,
or James 1:12–18.

When you _____ ,
read _____ .

Helping Others Make Positive Choices

Out of my love and concern for you, I give you this number to call in hope that you'll find help and support to stop your drinking.

Alcoholics Anonymous

_____

Out of my love and concern for you, I give you this number to call in hope that you'll find help and support to stop your drug use.

Narcotics Anonymous

_____

I have noticed lately that you are troubled by a loved one's use of alcohol or drugs. By calling the following number, you can find support and help.

Al-Anon

_____

I want you to know I care about you. If you ever have a problem or need someone to talk to, feel free to call me at any time.

_____

Phone # _____

A Disciple's Way of the Cross

First Station—Jesus Is Condemned.

"As for yourselves, beware; for they will hand you over to councils; and you will be beaten in synagogues; and you will stand before governors and kings because of me, as a testimony to them."

—*Mark 13:9*

Mohandas Gandhi was a lawyer who in the 1900s fasted in protest against the treatment of the untouchables in India and to end religious strife there. He was imprisoned on several occasions for his nonviolent protests to gain India's independence from Great Britain. Gandhi was assassinated on January 30, 1948.

Second Station—Jesus Takes His Cross.

[Jesus] called the crowd with his disciples, and said to them, "If any want to become my followers, let them deny themselves and take up their cross and follow me."

—*Mark 8:34; Matthew 16:24; Luke 9:23*

Arthur Ashe was an African American who broke into the white world of tennis. Ashe worked for racial equality. He challenged the government's weak efforts toward AIDS research after contracting AIDS from a blood transfusion. Arthur Ashe died in 1995 after a twelve-year battle with AIDS.

Third Station—Jesus Falls the First Time.

"Blessed are you when people revile you and persecute you and utter all kinds of evil against you falsely on my account."

—*Matthew 5:11*

Steven Biko fought against the apartheid system of South Africa. The government claimed he and others "accidentally fell down the steps or slipped on a bar of soap in the shower," which resulted in their death in 1977. The movie *Cry Freedom* is based on his life. Nelson Mandela spent twenty-eight years in jail for his stand against apartheid. He was released in 1990 and was elected president of South Africa on May 10, 1994.

Fourth Station—Jesus Meets His Mother.

"And the king will answer them, 'Truly I tell you, just as you did it to one of the least of these who are members of my family, you did it to me.'"

—*Matthew 25:40*

Mother Teresa of Calcutta founded the Sisters of the Missionaries of Charity, whose main mission is to teach the poor children, to nurse the sick, and to prepare the dying for a happy death. The sisters' work has expanded to the larger cities in the United States. Mother Teresa has received many awards including the Nobel Peace Prize in 1979.

Fifth Station—Jesus Is Helped by Simon of Cyrene.

"It will not be so among you; but whoever wishes to be great among you must be your servant . . . "

—*Matthew 20:26*

Amnesty International, a worldwide organization that involves musicians, actors, athletes, writers, teachers, students, doctors, and many others, acts on the conviction that governments must not deny individuals their basic human rights. Their main action on behalf of prisoners of conscience is through letter-writing campaigns.

Peace Troupe is a grassroots collective of artists, performers, and activists dedicated to nonviolent conflict resolution.

Sixth Station—Veronica Wipes the Face of Jesus.

"You are the light of the world. A city built on a hill cannot be hid. In the same way, let your light shine before others, so that they may see your good works and give glory to your Father in heaven."

—Matthew 5:14, 16

Jean Donovan, who, despite being from a privileged, successful family in Ohio, having a master's degree in economics and excellent career opportunities, decided in 1978 to join a team of missionaries in El Salvador to educate, feed, nurse, and wipe the faces of the many children of El Salvador. Jean Donovan and three missionary sisters were raped and shot in December 1980.

Seventh Station—Jesus Falls the Second Time.

"But before all this occurs, they will arrest you and persecute you; they will hand you over to synagogues and prisons, and you will be brought before kings and governors because of my name."

—Luke 21:12

Dorothy Day, a convert to Catholicism, was cofounder of the Catholic Worker Movement and a major figure in the Catholic peace movement and the growth of pacifism in the United States. Her commitment to social justice, especially to the poor, was evident by her six imprisonments for civil rights.

Eighth Station—Jesus Speaks to the Women of Jerusalem.

Then Jesus said, "Father, forgive them; for they do not know what they are doing."

—Luke 23:34

Rosa Parks led the civil rights crusade in 1955 by her refusal to give up her seat on a bus in Alabama. Susan B. Anthony worked for almost 60 years for women's right to vote in the United States. This right was granted in 1920 through the 19th amendment to the Constitution.

Ninth Station—Jesus Falls the Third Time.

"When they bring you to trial and hand you over, do not worry beforehand about what you are to say; but say whatever is given you at that time, for it is not you who speak, but the Holy Spirit."

—Mark 13:11

Christopher Reeve, Superman to many, is paralyzed from his neck down following an equestrian accident that happened in May 1995. He is an inspiration to all because of the value that he places on his life despite his paralysis. He is on the board of directors for the American Paralysis Association and is also supportive of the environment, AIDS, and other noteworthy causes.

Tenth Station—Jesus Is Stripped of His Garments.

"When they hand you over, do not worry about how you are to speak or what you are to say; for what you are to say will be given to you at that time. . . ."
—*Matthew 10:19*

Joan of Arc was an illiterate, teenage peasant girl who led French troops against English forces in 1430. She was taken prisoner and held in jail for about a year, where she was tried as a heretic, sentenced to death, and excommunicated. At the age of nineteen, she was burned at the stake. The Church canonized her a saint in 1920 and two years later declared her the patroness of France.

Eleventh Station—Jesus Is Nailed to the Cross.

"Very truly, I tell you, the one who believes in me will also do the works that I do and, in fact, will do greater works than these, because I am going to the Father."

—*John 14:12*

Martin Luther King Jr. was the voice of the nonviolent civil rights movement in the United States. From 1957 through January 1963, seventeen unsolved bombings of black churches and homes of civil rights leaders occurred. Lunch counter sit-ins and marches on city hall resulted in numerous arrests of Reverend King and other black people. Martin Luther King's belief was "nonviolence or nonexistence." He was assassinated on June 4, 1968.

Twelfth Station—Jesus Dies on the Cross.

"You have heard that it was said, 'You shall love your neighbor and hate your enemy.' But I say to you, Love your enemies and pray for those who persecute you. . . . "
—*Matthew 5:43–44*

Archbishop Oscar Romero of El Salvador, who because of his public announcements decrying the atrocities of the military forces in El Salvador, was put on the death list. On March 23, 1980, while saying Mass, Archbishop Romero was shot. No one has ever been found guilty or charged for his death nor the deaths of Jean Donovan and the three missionary sisters who were killed in December 1980.

Thirteenth Station—Jesus Is Taken Down from the Cross.

And Jesus said to him, "Foxes have holes, and birds of the air have nests; but the Son of Man has nowhere to lay his head."
—*Matthew 8:20*

Harriet Tubman was the "Moses" of her people, bringing black people out of slavery into freedom through the Underground Railroad system. She had $40,000 put out on her life because of her underground work.

Fourteenth Station—Jesus Is Placed in the Tomb.

"This is my commandment, that you love one another as I have loved you."
—*John 15:12*

Let us remember all who have worked for justice and for those who continue to work for justice but don't necessarily make the headlines—people like you and me who in our daily lives see wrongs and try to make right, those who proclaim the "gospel of life" to protect the least among us so that all may rise and enter the kingdom of heaven.

Prayers for Teenagers, by Teenagers

Dear God,

Thank you for all you have done for me. Today I ask for your guidance once more. As I start this day, I ask you to help me be my best, to be a friend despite all the difference we may have. Help us build our relationships based on truth and honesty. Amen.

—David Koch, age 14

Oh, Lord,

So often we forget to take the time to thank you. Throughout our busy days, with so many various activities, we neglect to say those three little words—Thank you, Lord.

Lord, this is not just a prayer of thanks, but also of petition. Help us remember to take the time to thank you for all that you have given us and all that you have done for us. Thank you, Lord. Amen.

—Doug Wessels, age 17

Dear Lord,

Thank you for the friends you gave me. They fill my life with joy and inspire me through the day. These friendships are ones that cannot be taken away. When I am down, I think about my friends and wipe away my frown. I want to thank You, Lord. You'll always be my friend.
 Amen.

—Heather Edgin, age 14

As sure as a baby will learn to run.
As sure as a father will love his son.
My love for you will grow, O Lord.
As sure as birds fill the air with song,
and bugs go on buzzing all night long.
My love for you will last, O Lord.
As sure as a mother cares for her child.
As sure as a kitten is soft and mild.
My love will never end, O Lord.
As long as the earth is spinning around,
to you, my Lord, I will be bound.
My love for you is ever, Lord.

—Mary Fangmann, age 13

Dear God,

Today I pray
everyone sees it your way.
That they don't judge people
by the color of the skin.
That they don't look on the outside,
but look at what is within.
That they're able to feel
everyone is their friend,
and the love they can share
will never, ever end.
I pray for the people
who just cannot see,
that everyone in the world
is in some way like you and me.
Amen.

—Jessica Osterhaus, age 12